1. Monolith, the Face of Half Dome, Yosemite. One of my earliest photographs (1926), this represented a 4000-foot climb with a 6½x8½ plate camera, and a magnificent bit of luck. I arrived not 30 minutes too soon for the fine distribution of sunlight on the 2000-foot sheer granite cliff of Half Dome. I was using Wratten Panchromatic Plates, and a 6½-inch Bausch and Lomb Tessar lens—uncoated of course—and in a very uncertain shutter. An F filter was used (Wratten No. 29). The exposure was fortunate—not many in those days were—and the developer was pyro. The progression of sky tones from horizon to zenith is interesting; even with a strong red filter a considerable area above the horizon is rendered very light. The snow has little or no textural values; in the print it is practically of Zones VIII to IX value. "Printing-down" results in a muddy gray.

NATURAL-LIGHT

PHOTOGRAPHY

ANSEL ADAMS

Basic Photo 4

MORGAN AND MORGAN, Inc. • **Hastings-on-Hudson, N.Y.**

THE FOUNTAIN PRESS, LONDON • **Agents for Great Britain**

"For data — the camera was faithfully used"
from *Fourth Sequence* (text)

Minor White, 1950

Recently some changes were made in the terminology of the Zone System, and are being applied in present writing and teaching. The basic principles of the Zone system remain unchanged and the new terms serve to clarify them. Throughout this book think of:

LUMINANCE	instead of Brightness
DENSITY VALUE	instead of Density Zone
PRINT VALUE	instead of Print Zone

The term ZONE remains the same when applied to Exposure Zone. Hence we can say: "LUMINANCE X, placed on EXPOSURE ZONE V and given Normal $+$ 1 development will yield DENSITY VALUE VI and PRINT VALUE VI." The term ZONE is limited to its true definition—an area on the Exposure Scale of the Negative. Hence, SUBJECT VALUES relate to PRINT VALUES as modified by our visualization and appropriate technical controls of placement, exposure and devolopment. LUMINANCES are measured in candles-per-square-foot (c/ft^2) (as per the dial of the Weston Meter). *It was not practical to make these changes throughout this book for this printing except in the definitions on page vii.* For application of the Zone System to the Polaroid Land Process refer to the new book by Ansel Adams, POLAROID LAND PHOTOGRAPHY MANUAL (Morgan and Morgan, Inc., Hastings-on-Hudson, N.Y. 10706).

I extend my appreciation and thanks to my many friends and associates who have helped so generously in the preparation of this book.

I dedicate these books to everyone who is interested in the development of straightforward photography and who believes in the simple statement of the lens.

The 5 *Basic Photo* books of this series by Ansel Adams are:

Book 1 *Camera & Lens; Studio, Darkroom, Equipment*
Book 2 *The Negative; Exposure and Development*
Book 3 *The Print; Contact Printing and Enlarging*
Book 4 *Natural-Light Photography*
Book 5 *Artificial-Light Photography*

Seventh Printing 1971

Printed and bound in U.S.A.

Library of Congress Catalog Card Number 48-2069.

iv

DESCRIPTION OF TERMS USED IN THIS BOOK

INTENSITY . . . . This refers to the light *source*, not to the light reflected from the subject.

INCIDENT LIGHT . . . The light falling upon a subject from a source of illumination—sun, sky, flash or photoflood lamps, reflector, etc.

REFLECTED LIGHT . . . . The light reflected from the subject to the spectator or the lens. My philosophy of photographic procedure is based on the evaluation of the light reflected from the subject and not on evaluation of the incident light. I support this philosophy on the basis of esthetic and emotional factors more than on physical considerations.

REFLECTANCE . . . A property of the subject; for example, "white marble has higher reflectance than red brick." Reflectance may be stated in percentage—Caucasian skin has a reflectance of 35%, black velvet of 2%, etc., signifying that these subjects reflect 35% and 2% respectively of the incident light falling upon them.

LUMINANCE . . . This refers to the light reflected from the subject: it is a property of both subject and lens image. It depends upon the intensity of the incident light and the reflectance of the subject.

BRIGHTNESS . . . A subjective interpretation of Luminance.

BRILLIANCY . . . . I use this term in relation to prints rather than the term *reflectance* (which is the technically accepted term). I do so because *brilliancy* is not only a quantitive term, but signifies emotional and esthetic qualities. It is the *arithmetic* equivalent of reflection density, which is a logarithmic value.

TRANSMISSION . . . . Transmission of a negative is that fraction of the light falling upon the negative which passes through it; if 4 units of light fall upon a given part of the negative and 2 units pass through the transmission is $\frac{1}{2}$ or 50%. But as we are more interested in the light-stopping power of the negative than in the light-transmitting power, we use the inverse of Transmission, which is—

OPACITY . . . This is defined as the reciprocal of the Transmission ($O = 1/T$). If the negative has a transmission in a given part of 1/10 or 10%, the Opacity is 10; if the transmission is $\frac{1}{4}$ or 25%, the Opacity is 4. Opacity, being an arithmetic value, is a simpler term which the nonscientific photographer can comprehend.

DENSITY . . . This is defined as the logarithm of the reciprocal of the transparency; that is, it is the logarithm of the opacity. In sensitometry, "density" is used in preference to "opacity" because it simplifies calculations and the plotting of the characteristic curves. It is measured on a densitometer, and *must* be expressed only in logarithmic terms. Its equivalent, opacity, is expressed only in arithmetic terms. Hence, we say "density 1.70" or its arithmetic equivalent (its antilog) "opacity 50."

It must be made clear that while *log density* and *arithmetic opacity* are interchangeable terms in the description of the light-stopping power of a negative, they represent different mathematical concepts, and in calculations are not interchangeable. Throughout this book I use the term *opacity* to represent the light-stopping powers of negatives: I use the term *density* only when necessary and then usually follow with the equivalent opacity value. I do not use the term "opacity" merely to create a new terminology, but because I am confident that the average person is not conversant with logarithms. It is much easier for him to comprehend the quantitative meaning of the phrase "opacity range of 1 to 25" than the phrase "density range of 1.40."

GAMMA . . . A value derived from the angle of the straight-line section of the D-log E curve in reference to the base which signifies the degree of contrast of the negative in relation to the contrast of the subject, and which is modified by the nature of the emulsion and the degree of development. Gamma is important in sensitometry and in color-separation work (color printing and reproduction). It has little or no meaning in practical black-and-white photography.

NOTE: The new terminology of the Zone System offers more logical definitions:

NEW TERMS	PREVIOUS TERMS
Subject Values	Subject Zones
Luminance (measured in c/ft^2)	Brightness
Density Values (negative)	Density Zones
Print Values (or Transparency Values)	Print Zones

COMPARISON TABLE
TRANSMISSION—DENSITY—OPACITY
A partial listing of comparative numbers.
Refer to the PHOTO-LAB-INDEX for fuller table.

Transmission	Density	Opacity	Transmission	Density	Opacity
1.0000	0.00	1.000	0.03162	1.50	31.62
0.9772	0.01	1.023	0.02512	1.60	39.81
0.7943	0.10	1.259	0.01995	1.70	50.12
0.6310	0.20	1.585	0.01585	1.80	63.10
0.5012	0.30	1.995	0.01259	1.90	79.43
0.3981	0.40	2.512	0.01000	2.00	100.00
0.3162	0.50	3.162	0.00794	2.10	125.9
0.2512	0.60	3.981	0.00631	2.20	158.5
0.1995	0.70	5.012	0.00501	2.30	199.5
0.1585	0.80	6.310	0.00398	2.40	251.2
0.1259	0.90	7.943	0.00316	2.50	316.2
0.10000	1.00	10.000	0.00251	2.60	398.1
0.07943	1.10	12.59	0.00199	2.70	501.2
0.06310	1.20	15.85	0.00158	2.80	631.0
0.05012	1.30	19.95	0.00125	2.90	794.3
0.03981	1.40	25.12	0.00100	3.00	1000.0

TABLE OF CONTENTS

Illustrations

2. Forest Detail, Yosemite. This is taken in full shade. The light tips of the branches were yellowish-green, the other parts of a rather deep green. The shadows in the deep forest were of very low value. This was made without a filter, with reduced exposure and prolonged development. The deepest tones were placed on Zone I, the lightest values were raised from Zones VI to Zone VIII. In this case there was no need for a green filter, as there were no other colors to differentiate. The contrast is but slightly related to color differences. The actual brightness range was about Zones I to VI; the reduced exposure and "normal-plus-plus" development expanded the range to about Zones I to VIII. In the original print some of the background tones are printed a deep black—more than a literal interpretation would allow. But the most distant tree trunks are not submerged in this "background" tone. It is true that the general illumination was bluish—from the open north sky—and that a blue filter (a very light one, such as the Zeiss Ikon B2 or a Wratten No. 38) might have slightly lightened the shadow values, but the same effect would obtain with more exposure and less development.

x

QUALITIES OF NATURAL LIGHT

Photography was conceived in natural light. Our visual reactions to the world about us are tied inexorably to the experience of the ages; by the process of evolution and adaptation our eyes have come to serve as instruments of perception and in some measure of interpretation, strengthening by association the other sensory impressions. Not only are objects perceived by daylight, but they are interpreted according to the direction, the intensity, and the color of the light. Hence the perceptual realities of the world largely depend upon the qualities of natural light. What are these qualities?

Direction

The dominant direction of daylight is from *above*, except for the brief periods near sunrise and sunset and in certain unusual angles of reflection, such as those from clouds, mountains, and buildings. Our basic impression of the sky as being above the earth and of all light as coming in a downward direction is too strongly fixed in consciousness to be overcome readily. Think of the appearance of practically everything about us in the out-of-doors; shapes, volumes, and planes are revealed and are recognizable as being lighted from above. When confronted with evidence of another direction of illumination we are required to make some mental adjustment. It may be a simple one or it may require definite effort, and it may produce pleasant or unpleasant reactions. The mood of "thunderstorm light," for example, may be dramatic and emotional; the light reflected horizontally through a long passageway may have bleak and disturbing qualities. Figures illuminated by a campfire appear quite logical when the campfire shows or is definitely suggested in the image. When the campfire does not appear, the lighting of the figures requires explanation. The spectator may be confused, although the person who made the picture accepts it without question.

We are all familiar with the unhappy results of the ordinary "passport photo." We say, "What a terrible likeness!" This response is largely because the illumination is flat, so that the planes and angles of the face are not revealed. The projected personality of the subject depends as much upon the complex relationship of these elements in his face as on the evidences of mobile expression, and a considerable mental and emotional adjustment is therefore necessary in order to "recognize" the subject of such a photograph. Of course, if we wish to create a departure from reality we can do so, but the results must be sufficiently telling to assure conviction; and it is difficult to depart convincingly from reality until reality itself is comprehended.

Color

Sunlight and skylight combined give us "daylight." Obviously, the color of daylight is modified by a number of factors: the proportion of direct sunlight to skylight, the angle of the sun, the area and the nature of clouds, and the color of the immediate environment. The color quality *of light* has major significance in color photography, but it also concerns us to some degree in black-and-white photography in regard to the use of filters and to the color sensitivity of our emulsions. This color quality of light is called *color temperature*, and the term is properly used in reference to the light emitted by "black-body" light sources (sun, tungsten lamp, wood fire, etc.).

1

Technically, it is expressed in degrees Kelvin (°K), which are the same as Centigrade degrees plus 273° (absolute zero is—273°C.) For example, if a piece of iron were heated to 800° Centigrade, the light emitted therefrom would have a color temperature of 1073°K. Light from the sun and from tungsten lamps has true color temperature, but light from the sky, gaseous discharge tubes, fluorescent lamps, etc. cannot be accurately evaluated in terms of color temperature; with such sources the term is used only in the most approximate way. Hence in relation to daylight I will not use the term, but refer to the light as being "warm" (low color temperature), or "cold" (high color temperature). It is important to remember that our eyes accommodate themselves quickly to moderate differences in color temperature; under ordinary conditions we "see" only rather extreme differences of color temperatures—such as sunrise or sunset colors—but we are not aware of the "blueness" or the "coldness" of an overcast sky that is so apparent in a color photograph.

I experienced a spectacular demonstration of the visual differences of tungsten light and daylight when, after I had spent an hour or so in an art gallery entirely illuminated by tungsten light, a door was opened at the far end revealing a park vista in late afternoon light. My eyes had become so accustomed to the tungsten illumination that I was not in any way conscious of its relative "warmth" until a small section of the field of view (the door) was seen under "cold" daylight. The exterior scene appeared as a startling blue; flowers and trees were all suffused with a strong bluish cast. I immediately went outside; the illusion of blue soon vanished and objects took on a "normal" color quality. On looking back to the interior of the gallery everything seemed under a golden glow; when I returned to the gallery, the adaptation was again made, and objects appeared "normal" in color. The photographic film can make no such adaptation as the eye—color film is especially sensitive to small changes in color temperature. Hence when we visualize images we cannot discount the effect of the color of the light, although we must know that it is difficult to evaluate visually even generous differences of color temperature (except by direct comparison).

In black-and-white photography considerable control of values is possible under various conditions of lighting by the use of proper films and filters. Panchromatic film, having relatively low sensitivity to blue, gives an image of rather strong contrasts, especially when a yellow filter is used. An orthochromatic film gives a softer image with the same filter, since its lower sensitivity to orange will lower the color values of the objects directly illuminated, and its higher relative sensitivity to blue will give a proportionately stronger image of the shadows. Minimum contrast can be achieved by using a blue filter, which will lower the values of the objects directly illuminated and strongly raise the shadow values.

A filter has maximum transmission of its own color; blue surfaces, bluish haze or smoke, etc. will always be rendered lighter by a blue filter. Red surfaces, reddish haze or sunset clouds, etc. will always be rendered lighter with a red filter.

As we shall see later, the control of shadow values is of tremendous importance in all outdoor photography. However, we need not concern ourselves at this point with evaluation of color temperature in black-and-white photography, beyond this recognition of its general significance. Knowing the principles involved will enable us to comprehend and clarify many otherwise perplexing problems. This subject is expanded in the chapter on filters.

2

The intensity of natural light is of course of tremendous range. The drop from the strong sunlight at high altitudes to the diffuse low light in a deep forest may represent a scale of from one to many thousand units of light intensity. The reflective qualities of various surfaces modify the values of the light, some substances reflecting more, some less, of a given incident light. In Book 2 we considered the difference between incident and reflected light, stressing the fact that subjects are actually photographed by reflected light, which can be read directly with the conventional photoelectric exposure meter, such as the Weston Master Meter (my personal choice). For precise work the S.E.I. Exposure Photometer is unequaled (see Book 2). The Heiland Pentax 3°/21 meter is an excellent device.

Meters such as the English S.E.I. Exposure Photometer give much more precise evaluation of the brightness of small areas than do the conventional photoelectric meters. The Weston, for example, covers an angle of about 30°; the S.E.I. can measure an angle of only 1°—roughly, an object 4 inches in diameter at a distance of 35 feet. The Gamma Scientific, Inc., Luminance Analyzer a-500 EC measures with great accuracy a solid angle of $\frac{1}{2}$°.

It is extremely important that the exposure meter be read properly. In Book 2 it is shown that the meter responds to the average brightness of light from a field the extent of which is determined by the angle view of the meter. In reading a shadow area it is imperative to see that the field of the meter does not include extraneous bright areas; otherwise the readings will be too high. Conversely, in reading bright areas it is imperative to be certain that the field of the meter does not include extraneous dark areas; otherwise the reading will be too low.

Most exposure failures result from erroneous meter readings.

The average outdoor scene is illuminated by light from two general sources—sun and sky, alone or combined. The intensity of this light varies with season, latitude, atmospheric conditions, time of day, and altitude. Although exposure tables have been devised that take account of a number of conditions—surmised light intensity, light direction, character of subject, etc., as well as film speed—it is impossible to estimate the variables reliably, and such tables are inadequate for carefully controlled work. Film speeds and lens stops are reasonably consistent. Shutter speeds are very erratic; shutters should be checked and the *actual* speeds determined at frequent intervals. The unaided eye is not a good judge of the intensity of incident or reflected light. Of course, with long experience we can satisfactorily estimate direct and reflected light intensities within certain limits, but we can never be *sure*. For precise control, use an exposure meter.

We can do little if anything to modify the basic values of natural light. We must therefore learn how to make the best use of it, modifying method if we cannot control illumination. We must understand how the range of brightness of a subject often depends largely upon the reflective qualities of the subject itself as well as on the intensity of the source light. For example, dark and light cards may reflect 50 and 1000 units of light respectively in sunlight, and 5 and 100 units of light under skylight; the *range* of reflected values is the same in both cases—1:20. However, if the dark card is placed under skylight and the light card in sunlight, the range is 1:200, and if the placements are reversed the range is only 1:2!

3

Thus in a normal landscape under daylight we are confronted with a wide brightness range that is determined not only by the nature of the subject but also by the relative intensities of sunlight and skylight. On overcast days, or when the subject is placed entirely in shade (skylight), this range is greatly reduced. In addition we may have areas of the subject that are shielded from both sunlight and skylight and illuminated only by light reflected by other parts of the subject. The brightness of such areas is usually very low. Lest the foregoing appear unnecessarily obvious, it should be pointed out that too few photographers are fully aware of what light values can mean in both practical and emotionally expressive terms. Awareness of the subject-brightness range is essential to adequate visualization of the final photograph. After all, it is the light coming to your lens from the subject that you record on the film!

The clearer the air, the more intense the light from the sun and the less intense the skylight, and therefore the greater the difference between sunlit and shadowed areas. In mountain photography, exposure of average scenes must usually be increased at higher altitudes, rather than decreased, if shadow values are to be rendered adequately. Of course if shadow areas are few and small, so that detail is not important in them, the opposite is true, but in the majority of outdoor scenes there is a rather large amount of shadow area that needs clear rendition. On the other hand, in regions where the air is laden with smoke and haze from industry, the intensity of the sun's rays is reduced, while reflection from the sky is increased. Also, when the sky contains light clouds or haze, the shadows are more strongly illuminated and the ratio of sunlight to skylight is decreased. Less contrast results; you can compensate with less exposure and *more* development.

3. Leaves, Owens Valley, California. Problem similar to that of Figure 2. An excellent decorative subject.

On hilltops, on the sea, on pavements, and on open plains, you find the light composed chiefly of sunlight and skylight, although secondary reflected light from earth or water may be considerable, and from an opposite direction. On snow or white sand, for example, environmental reflections are usually very strong. Near-by objects of high reflectivity lighten the shadows, often to an extent that may be perplexing to the spectator of the finished print if the reflecting object does not show in the field of view. Near-by dark objects, such as trees, dark rocks, or buildings, modify the shadows by *cutting off* light from part of the sky; it is false to think of dark objects as "absorbing" light from the subject. Environmental reflections have no appreciable effect on sunlit areas of the subject, but may have profound effect on the shadows. This is of great concern to color photographers, since green trees, red walls, and so forth may reflect obvious colors into the shadows of the subject. This effect is quite different from the effect produced by lens flare, which creates a cast of the dominant color over the entire image. An expanse of blue sky within the field of the lens, if not in the field of the picture, will be reflected by the air-glass surfaces of the lens and create a bluish cast over the entire image. For this reason I urgently advise coated lenses for color photography. As of now (1965) practically all lenses are coated.

It is necessary to stress again that the eye automatically compensates for differences of brightness and color in the subject, perceiving a more refined color

4. Tenaya Lake, Yosemite (from *Yosemite and the Sierra Nevada*, Houghton Mifflin Co., Boston). Wratten G filter used. Shadow on mountain within Zones I-III range; sunlight on distant peak about Zone IX.

5

range and a greater brightness range than can be registered on any film. The only way to accurately determine effective subject brightnesses is by measurement with an exposure meter and a consideration of emotional as well as actual tone-relationships in visualizing your final print.

We are frequently astonished by the difference between our visual impressions and what the light meter indicates. Also, if we use a monochromatic viewing filter (such as the Wratten No. 90), we will be surprised to observe unexpected contrasts (or lack of contrasts) of subject colors in terms of black-and-white values.

It is advisable here to clarify the reflectivity range of subjects. With a single consistent source of illumination, black velvet reflects about 2% of the incident light, and a surface of magnesium oxide about 96%. This represents a reflectivity range of 1:48—approximately the maximum possible reflectivity range of ordinary substances. (The black silver deposit of a glossy photographic print in relation to the white paper base will suggest a range of 1:50 or more, but such heavy light-absorbing surfaces are seldom if ever found in nature.) But once we have a variety of illumination on a subject, we increase its contrast or reflectivity range. For example, the sunlight-and-shadow brightness ratio as reflected from a gray card in my garden is 1:8. Therefore a subject of maximum reflectivity range of 1:40 in direct sunlight (or in open skylight), when photographed in sunlight *and* skylight, would present a reflectivity (brightness) range of 1:320. And if parts of the subject shield other parts from both sunlight and skylight, the reflectivity of the shielded areas is further lowered and the total contrast or brightness range is increased. From my window I see a bright painted house in sunlight and some earth under a near-by plant in shade. The brightness range as determined by the S.E.I. meter is 1:2500! To evaluate the brightness range of this subject by measuring incident light alone would be quite impracticable, as so many *differences of illumination* must be considered.

Sunlight

Sunlight differs from ordinary artificial light in more than the basic physical properties, such as intensity and color. The revelation of form, volume, texture, and color possible in sunlight should be fully recognized and utilized. These qualities are determined not only by the differences between sunlight and shadow brightness in the same subject, but by the angle of the sun to the planes of the subject and, less well understood by most photographers, by the quality of the shadow edge. The quality of the shadow edge is related to the effective width of the light source; that is, the angle subtended by its diameter. The shadow edge loses sharpness and becomes broader as this angle becomes greater. The sun subtends $\frac{1}{2}°$ of arc; were this angle larger, the shadow edge at a given distance from the shadowing object would be broader and more indefinite. Were the angle smaller, the shadow edge would be sharper. In fact, point-source lights (electric arcs, etc.) produce sharp shadows even when the shadowing edge is at a great distance from the shadowed surface.

Beams of collimated light, such as those from some spotlights, also cast sharp-edged shadows. To reproduce artificially a shadow edge like that formed by sunlight would require an uncollimated light source of such diameter and distance from the subject as to subtend $\frac{1}{2}°$ of arc.

6

Sunlight quality is recognized not only by its shadow edge but also by the acuteness of highlights. A broad light source produces a broad highlight, a point source produces a small, sharp highlight (see Book 3, p. 23). Thus a variation of the angle subtended by the diameter of the light source modifies the highlights of the subject as well as its shadow edges. As the direct rays of the sun are progressively veiled by light clouds or haze, the shadow edge becomes more diffuse; under an overcast sky or an open sky without sun, the shadow edge attains maximum diffusion.

We can think of sunlight as the "main" light and skylight as the "enveloping" light. Reflectors may be used (see page 92) when additional light in the shadows is required, but the obvious addition of any directional light, either sharp or diffused, may destroy the mood of actuality unless most carefully controlled (see chapter on Synchro-sunlight).

Analyzing the effect of sunlight on various objects proves the importance of the angle of illumination in revealing forms, planes, and textures. If the direction of the sunlight coincides with the optical axis of the lens, a subject appears without shadow, but the shadow of the camera is in the center of the field. A practical "axis" light, if it is wanted, is achieved by bringing the axis of the lens as close as possible to the direction of the sun *without* including the shadow of the camera anywhere in the field of view.

5. Refugio Beach, California (from *Portfolio One*). Taken directly into sun. Glare on water and wet sand partially on Zone IX in print; its brightness approached 4000 c.p.sq.ft. Dark rocks at about 6.5 c.p.sq.ft. were placed on Zone I, high values on Zone IX and above. The negative contained more values than are used in the print; the image is intentionally "printed down" (see Book 3) to achieve the desired mood.

A plane surface under axis light reflects equally from all parts of its area, a curved surface reflects the maximum light from the area nearest the light, with the intensity diminishing as the surface curves away from the plane perpendicular to the rays. Under this direction of sunlight forms are revealed not by strong combinations of areas of light and shade, but by subtle variations within fully illuminated areas. As we approach the edge of the curve, most of the light is reflected away from the camera, and if the object is against a light background, its edge appears quite dark. This is known as the *limb effect*. A light form against a dark background presents a somewhat indefinite edge, as the dark limb merges into the dark background. Figure 6 shows an egg photographed in axis light against a light background. Figure 7 represents a practical application of this type of lighting, demonstrating a remarkable interpretation of line and form under axis light. The qualities of axis lighting are clearly perceived by the eye, and can be minimized or exaggerated in the photograph by control of exposure and development. It should be emphasized that axis light minimizes textural effects if we consider texture to be represented by minute, sharp differentiations of light and shade (see page 31).

6. Egg in axis light. Taken with afternoon sun on camera axis; shadow of camera within about 1-inch of base of egg. Background was white mounting board of almost similar brightness value. Contrast exaggerated by reduced exposure and prolonged development.

7. Nude on Sand (by Edward Weston). This is a magnificent example of "axis" lighting. Forms are revealed by variation of line and surface values rather than by juxtapositions of masses of light and shade. It is a perfect example of the "limb" effect (the pun is unintentional!). With axis lighting we can photograph white against white, delineating the forms by use of the simple "limb" effect. Increased contrast is usually implied.

What is almost the opposite of axis lighting is termed *back lighting*, and the problems involved are of both esthetic and technical nature. Most substances when illuminated by a sharp angle of light from behind reflect both diffuse and specular light of very high brightness value. The parts of the subject toward the camera are mostly in shadow, and even if these shadowed areas are of relatively high brightness, the exceptional brightness of the directly illuminated edges makes them appear of very low value. Let us suppose we are making a portrait "into the sun"; we are in a highly reflective environment of bright sand and sky, so the brightness of the shadowed areas of the head is 50 c.p.sq.ft. The back-lighted illumination on hair, cheek, and shoulder may approach 1000 c.p.sq.ft. If the shadowed brightness is placed on Zone IV, the high values would fall between Zones VIII and IX. Actually, to show adequate texture, the high values should have their highest placement between VII and VIII; that would mean the shadow values would fall on Zone III. The resulting image would be disappointing, as the mood of the light would not be conveyed. While back lighting produces high actual contrast, the *mood* is one of enveloping light; the eye sees into the shadow values. A face is not a dark mass surrounded by a halo of light. Hence the shadow values should not be placed lower than Zone V—sometimes as high as Zone VI— and the high values should be controlled by adequate development procedure.

9

In axis sunlight the brightness scale of a subject is quite short (except for possible minute shadow areas, which will be rendered dark), so that expansion of values in exposure and processing is usually indicated. This is also somewhat true in a photograph made wholly in the shade or on a gray day, although the actual brightnesses here are low compared to those in sunlight. There is one important difference between axis light from the sun and diffuse skylight. The latter casts a broad and diffuse but appreciable shadow, whereas in axis sunlight practically all parts of the subject are bathed in light.

It is very important that the lowest values in a subject in shade be evaluated and placed upon the exposure scale properly. The mood of diffuse light is usually one of enveloping rather than directional light; all parts of the subject are almost uniformly revealed to the eye. If the lowest values are rendered black in the photograph, this illusion of enveloping light may be lost, so that a harsh, dead quality results. Of course there are always small shadows that can be rendered black in the print, but larger areas in which substance and texture are important should also be properly brought out.

8. Roots. Subjects of this general character—involved forms of considerable depth—usually have a rather unexpected high brightness range. The nearest parts of the subject were exposed to the open sky; the deepest parts were heavily shaded, and the exposure range was at least 1:64. It frequently happens that a smooth surface of wood will show a high semispecular reflection.

While the literal values of a scene in shade may be of fairly close contrast range, almost without exception an expansion of the contrast range in the negative is called for. Since impressions of both light and substance are essential, these slight contrasts must be exaggerated—though not to the point where the lowest important ones are obscured nor the highest are blocked. Exposure placement should be carefully studied; the opalescent qualities of subtle tones in diffuse light are lost if exposure is too great or development is carried beyond the optimum for a conservatively low exposure placement.

We must remember that shadow light has, under almost all conditions, a relatively high color temperature (that is "cold," tending toward blue). With orthochromatic film, therefore, brightnesses of shadow areas produce about the same *proportionate* densities in the negative as do similar surfaces in sunlight. With panchromatic emulsions, however, with their slightly lower sensitivity to blue light, I am inclined to place shadow readings about one-half zone higher on the exposure scale than "normal" placement might be. This is a personal application; I know of no reference elsewhere to the subject. I suggest that you make careful comparative tests and determine for yourself the applicability of this method to your own work.

The use of filters on subjects in full shade has considerable effect. The exposure factors of yellow, green, and red filters must be increased under these conditions, and the factors for blue filters decreased. In fact, the use of blue filters when photographing objects in strong light and shade reduces otherwise harsh contrasts to a gratifying degree. The chapter on filters makes the reason for this clear.

With uncoated lenses there is always the danger that flare light from the sky may veil the image. A lens hood may be more useful on a gray day than on a bright, sunny one, as the intensity of the sky may greatly exceed the brightnesses of the subject itself. If no sky is involved, of course flare is not a problem, though it should be understood that sky need not appear within the field of view to produce a flare effect; sky areas within 80° of the optical axis can produce flare. If the front surface of a lens is dirty or scratched, the flare is increased tremendously—it may even ruin the image. And of course if sun strikes the lens surface, flare is increased. A clean, well-polished lens and a lens hood of maximum length (though not long enough to cut the corners of the field) are essential if the lens is not coated.* The possibility of flare *within the camera* (reflection from bellows and frame), must not be overlooked (see Book 1, p. 112).

---

* I cite two cases of flare effect—in each case the photographer did not know of flare as a property of the optical system, but was aware of its effect. Several years ago a motion-picture photographer was perplexed because when he used an optical-flat neutral-density filter to reduce exposure he obtained a higher shadow value in relation to highlight value than when he reduced exposure by simply using a smaller aperture. Paul Strand found he obtained a smoother negative with his Cooke lens than with a Dagor. Neither person could explain the reason for this effect, nor could I; at that time there was scant mention of the subject in photographic literature. The cause of reduced image contrast lay in the addition of the two air-glass surfaces of the neutral-density filter to the optical system of the motion-picture camera, and in the fact that the Cooke lens had six or eight air-glass surfaces in comparison with the four air-glass surfaces of the Dagor. The increased flare from the extra reflecting surfaces actually added density to the negative (apparent in the shadow and other low-value areas), "smoothing out" the contrast *difference* between the high-value and the shadow areas.

We know that even light from the open sky is directional. Not only is it generally from above, but there is more light from some parts of the sky than from others. This subtle difference of intensity should be considered, as the delicate back-lighting effects it can produce will enhance the revelation of form and space.

There is no more beautiful illumination than that from open sky alone, including overcast and fog; it is favorable to the accurate rendition of related tones and colors that is so necessary in copying works of art, fabrics, etc. For portraiture and the minutiae of nature it is exquisite, though interpretation naturally presents many problems. Not only must the print reveal a subtle gradation—be neither thin nor harsh—but the print color (see Book 3) is a major expressive factor in the interpretation of subjects under this lighting.

We should guard against unexpected high contrasts, and not take for granted that subjects under diffused light or in shade are always "soft." In intricate subjects, such as "Roots" (Fig. 8), there are deeply recessed areas of very low brightness values. Likewise, the heavy shadows from hat brims, in sockets of deep-set eyes, and areas under stones and logs, etc. should not be overlooked.

9. Silver Gate, Yellowstone National Park. A composition of white rocks and white sky (panchromatic film but no filter) and a mountain in shade. With a blue filter the mountain would be lighter in tone.

In mixed lighting the reflective values of the subject are modified by the extremes of light intensity; a subject of diffuse reflective surface appears roughly eight times as bright under sunlight as under open skylight. In high altitudes, under deep-blue skies this ratio is increased; at sea level, where heavy atmosphere, mist, haze, and fog are prevalent, the ratio decreases. Environmental reflective effects are unpredictable, since, as we have noted, nearby brilliant objects decrease the ratio and dark objects, such as rocks, foliage, and dark buildings, increase it. A typical example would be a figure standing in a shaft of sunlight in a dense grove of trees. In this case the ratio between sunlit skin and deep forest shadow might approximate 1:1600 or more. Errors of judgment on such a full range of values are inevitable, because the eye has a far greater adaptability to extremes of brightness than does the photographic film. And of course the color of the light illuminating the shadows has a profound effect on the photographic response.

Technically, a combination of sunlight and shade presents the most serious problems to the photographer. Expressively, the problem is not so difficult; with both sun and shadow a more realistic interpretation is implied. Procedures favoring normal or compacted values are usually indicated, according to the values desired in the shadow areas.

10. Road, Owens Valley, California, Autumn. Autumn foliage, intensified by using a G filter. In the original print detail is retained in the shadows. Taken against the sun; the sky holds a fairly high value.

13

The chief problem is to preserve the *illusion of light* falling upon the subject. A print intended to convey an emotional impression may differ from a normal photographic record. You must visualize the final expressive print, expose for the desired values of the shadows, and control the high values by development. Average meter readings of the usual sun-and-shadow scenes are seldom adequate for the best placements of values on the expressive scale. Of course, what is "adequate" depends on the individual photographer's visualization of his final print.

Everyone knows how often a photograph suggests a "lunar" quality: the dark skies, the empty shadows, and the overintense high values (see Fig. 11). Careless use of filters augments this effect. Except for intentional dramatic effects, it is usually desirable to reveal substance in both sunlit and shadowed areas of the subject, so that the illusion of enveloping light is preserved and the emotional progression of values is logical—no matter in what general level of tone the print is conceived. A preponderance of heavy black shadow masses, obscuring surface and substance in the print image, betrays the superficial photographer. Nevertheless, when intelligently employed to develop design ideas and decorative patterns, such effects may be entirely justified. Edward Weston's magnificent sand-dune pictures are examples worthy of study in this respect; the intense black areas become eloquent because of their function in the rhythm and the design of the photograph. I believe there is a general agreement that black, empty shadows are better tolerated than blocked-up, textureless high values.

11. Adobe Church, New Mexico. An example of "lunar" quality; superficially dramatic tonalities.

14

The element of design—photographic design—is of extreme importance in visualization of the image. Great enthusiasm for the subject sometimes veils a clear concept of the image of it! An exciting subject, such as a cluster of fine farm buildings, may exist in an environment of space of field and sky, but in the print this "space" may appear as dull, neutral areas of distressingly low interest. Space in nature is one thing: space confined and restricted by the picture edges is quite another thing. Space and shape must be made eloquent—not in imitation of ordinary painting arrangements (as with so much "pictorial" photography) but in terms of the living camera image. Design, form, tone, and texture must all be considered together in a sensitive visualization of a photograph.

12. Saguaro Cactus, Arizona. This was photographed with a green filter (Zeiss-Ikon 55G). The effect on the sky is about the same as with a K2 filter, but the green of the cactus is intensified.

13. Half Dome, Autumn Tree, Yosemite. Taken "against the sun." The cliff is in shade, and the sky is quite light (the exposure was rather full, and development slightly less than normal). A G filter was used, rendering the oak leaves quite high in value. The inherent contrast was high—sunlit leaves against shadowed cliffs. If these leaves were competing with other sunlit areas, or were just against the sky, some intensification of contrast would have been indicated. exposure would have been reduced and development prolonged (one zone less exposure and normal-plus development).

LIGHT: REFLECTION AND COLOR

White, Gray, and Black

If the light falling upon a subject is of average spectral quality (say mean noon sunlight at Washington, D.C.), any substance that strongly reflects *all* wavelengths or colors of this incident light in equal proportion is recognized as white. It is not white, however, unless it has a high brightness (reflects most of the incident light). A surface of magnesium oxide, for example, may reflect 98% of the incident light; the reflected spectrum is the same as the spectrum of the incident white light, and the surface therefore appears both bright and white. Whiteness is, to some extent, a function of brightness, because even though a substance may reflect all the incident wavelengths or colors of light, if it reflects them at appreciably reduced intensity, its color is recognized as gray. What we call black is usually only a very deep gray. Black velvet is not truly black; it reflects some light—perhaps 2% or 3% of the incident light.* However, if it reflects or absorbs equally all bands of the incident-light spectrum, it does not give an impression of color. What constitutes the difference between black, white, and neutral gray tones, then, is the amount of light reflected, neutral grays and black being merely lessened reflections of white light. However, you must not overlook the psychological appreciation of whiteness; once you *know* a piece of paper is white, the conviction of its whiteness remains, no matter what the illuminating conditions may be. Visualization of image values is based on relative, not absolute, brightnesses. Take several identical pieces of white paper and place them at progressively greater distances from a light source (such as a small window in a large room); for the sake of clear description assume that the papers are placed at 4, 8, 12, and 16 feet from the window. The relative brightnesses will be 1, $\frac{1}{4}$, $\frac{1}{9}$, and $\frac{1}{16}$ in relation to distances from the window. (These values will be slightly modified by reflections from walls and ceilings, but for all practical purposes you can assume the 1:16 brightness difference will apply.) The paper nearest the window appears the brightest and the most distant paper the grayest, but you *know* all the papers are the same, hence you appreciate all of them as *white*, and you recognize that the differences in value are due to differences of illumination. In visualizing the photograph of the papers, the first one would obviously be Zone VIII or above and the most distant paper would fall approximately on Zone IV. Now if you move farther from the window and face the second paper, it will appear white, and if photographed will be of Zone VIII value. The third paper will be about two-fifths as bright and the fourth paper one-fourth as bright. If you stand before the third paper (long enough to accustom your eyes to the reduced brightness at this point) you will recognize it as *white*, and the fourth paper as only slightly less bright (about four-sevenths, to be exact). And finally, the fourth paper, when viewed alone, you will see and accept as white.

---

* See Book 2, p. 21.

Assume that the wall against which all the papers are seen is quite dark (intrinsically and because of its distance from the window—same as No. 4); if the wall has only one-fourth the reflectivity of the paper, its relative zonal position to each of the four visualizations—together with the relative zonal values of the papers—will be *approximately:*

	Zones Which the Various Papers Represent				Wall	Brightness Range
1st paper	VIII	VI	IV-V	IV	II	1:64
2nd paper	—	VIII	VII—	VI	IV	1:16
3rd paper	—	—	VIII	VII+	V+	1:8+
4th paper	—	—	—	VIII	VI	1:4

The above example has many implications in the practice of photography in natural light. Some of these are:

1. In photographing interiors with window light alone, a marked falling-off of brightness is inevitable.

2. In photographing objects in extremes of light and shade, your visualization must be very objective; the adaptability of the eye gives false impressions of brightness.

For example, I am photographing a person against a large tree; tree and figure are in shade, in the distance is a bright, sunny landscape. My eye appreciates this scene without difficulty. I am reminded of the exquisite early Italian paintings in which the near figures and the distant landscape are revealed with luminosity and precision. I "see" the final print in which the complex of values of the figure and the tree and the complex of values of the distant landscape are rendered with the clarity and the balance that my eye perceives. But when I measure the actual brightnesses with a good meter, I find that the brightness range is extreme, and severely taxes the exposure range of the film. But note this: The total range of brightness (say 1:120) can be recorded on the film merely as brightnesses; the emotional importance of the brightnesses is quite another thing. Assume the brightnesses are (in c.p.sq.ft.):

In Shade:	White dress	100	*In Sun:*	Sky	300
	Skin	25		Clouds	800
	Tree trunk	6.5		Hills	200
				Foliage	100

Brightness range in shade . . . . about 1:15
Brightness range in sun . . . . about 1:8
Full brightness range . . . . about 1:120

If you place the tree trunk on Zone I, the clouds will fall on Zone VIII; physically, the brightnesses lie within the exposure range of the film. Unfortunately, with this placement the skin values fall on Zone III and the white dress falls on Zone V. Emotionally, this is quite inadequate. The white dress, even in shade, "feels" white, and in the photograph it must also "feel" white. The skin values in full shade cannot fall below Zone V and retain a quality of substance and light. The average values of the tree trunk likewise cannot be placed below Zone III. Hence you must place your brightnesses on the exposure range somewhat as follows:

Tree trunk	in shade	(6.5)	. . . .	Zone	III
Skin values	in shade	(25)	. . . .	Zone	V
White dress	in shade	(100)	. . . .	Zone	VII
Foliage	in sun	(100)	. . . .	Zone	VII
Hills	in sun	(200)	. . . .	Zone	VIII
Sky		(300)	. . . .	Zone	VIII-IX
Clouds		(800)	. . . .	Zone	X

Obviously, this calls for definite development control. Personally, I would use the two-solution formula (page 78) as the most effective means of combining the two fields of brightnesses into a satisfactory range of image values. In any event the controls cannot achieve a perfect emotional balance, because each field of brightness should be interpreted within the full range of image values to convey the emotional scale of values that the eye perceives. Accordingly some compromise must be made. I would feel that the near figure should be given emphasis. If the white dress and the skin values in shade are adequately rendered, the mind can adjust the values of the distant view into some semblance of emotional reality; but it would be difficult to capture the mood of light and substance were tree, skin, and dress rendered too deep in tone. Of course, with the proper use of reflectors and/or flash fill-in, the extremes of brightness could be overcome. A fill-in of more than two zones is unsatisfactory; the quality of the fill-in light becomes obviously different from the quality of the natural light.

3. When photographing white objects (such as shells, white rocks) in flat skylight, you must remember that in flat light the brightness values are proportionate to the reflectivity of the objects, and your results may be disappointingly soft unless you achieve the desired contrast by proper exposure and development. For example, a white shell against gray rocks would present a reflectivity range of say 20% and 80%, or 1:4. The shell, being an emotionally white, translucent object, you would visualize as a Zone VII-VIII value, and the rocks as about a Zone IV value. If you place the rocks on Zone IV, the shell will fall on Zone VI. Hence, to preserve the "feel" of whiteness, the exposure might be based on Zone IV for the rocks and a normal-plus development would expand the opacity range sufficiently to yield a Zone VII-VIII value for the shell. Any light, translucent object may possess a brightness range within itself of as much as 1:4; the *impression* of translucent whiteness is complex and is obtained as much from the interplay of light *within* the substance as from the reflection of light from its surface. Hence such a subject must never be rendered as a "chalky," blank white.

Color

Suppose, however, that an object reflects roughly 50% of the light falling on it, but does not reflect all wavelengths equally. It may, for example, absorb little more of the blue and green wavelengths than of the yellow; it reflects some light in which yellow predominates, and the object appears to the eye as somewhat yellowish-gray. We speak of it as a yellow of low saturation.

Another object may reflect but little white light, absorbing almost everything except the blue wavelengths; it appears to the eye as a strong blue, and we refer to it as a blue of high saturation. The more white light such an object reflects along with the dominant blue light, the paler (grayer) the blue and the lower the color saturation.

19

Objects in nature reflect varying amounts of unabsorbed white light along with the characteristic color. This is a very important fact that must be thoroughly understood; full color saturation means a total purity of color, and must not be expected in natural reflective surfaces. Practically all the substances of the natural world reflect complex colors. In foliage, for example, the predominant color is green, but it is not the pure green of one particular wavelength in the spectrum; there are many other colors mixed with it. For your purposes it will suffice to consider that any color not fully saturated is admixed with a certain amount of reflected white light as well as the color of the light that predominates. Remember that "reflected white light" may impress you visually as gray, since neutral gray is only a depressed intensity of reflected white light.

Again, the apparent (visual) color of an object may result from a color complex that would require a spectroscopic analysis to describe. For example, blue and red together comprise magenta to the eye; nonpanchromatic film would respond to the blue component only, while panchromatic film would respond to both red and blue. The higher the percentage of red, the darker it would be rendered on nonpanchromatic film, the lighter on a red-sensitive one. Hence variations that are not too noticeable to the eye may become startlingly accentuated when rendered in black, grays, and white with various types of film.

14. Mount McKinley, Alaska (from *Portfolio One*). The reddish sunrise color suffused both snow and sky, and a deep yellow or a red filter would not have had much effect. A No. 12 filter was used, chiefly to reduce the shadowed foreground values and the sky value *above* the summit of the mountain.

FILM RESPONSE AND FILTERS

Photographic films, unfortunately, do not respond to color in the same way as the human eye. In general, films are more sensitive to the shorter wavelengths (blue and violet) than to the longer ones (red). The old-fashioned "color-blind" emulsion does not respond to green, yellow, or red at all. That is why foliage or red surfaces appear very dark in old-time collodion plates; the image has been made on the negative only by the blue and violet light reflected from the object, and if the red or green areas show any density at all, it is because of the blue or violet wavelengths reflected from these areas along with the predominant visual color.

The sky appears blue because of the scattering of the blue light from the sun by the minute particles in the atmosphere. Likewise blue light is scattered and absorbed by the emulsion of the negative. A negative made with blue light (such as when a Wratten C5 filter is used) is always softer than one made with green, red, or white light: the blue rays scatter and do not penetrate as far into the emulsion. Green rays scatter less and penetrate more than blue, but not as much as red rays. Hence photographs made with red filters always show a higher "gamma," or contrast, for any degree of development. To achieve optimum contrast, if we consider the correct development for a green-filter image as "normal", then we must give "less-than-normal" for the red-filter image, and "more-than-normal" for the blue filter image. This contrast effect is distinct from the color sensitivity of the film. Orthochromatic film is not sensitive to red light; it responds only to green and blue, and (as do all emulsions) to violet and ultra-violet light.

A filter is primarily a device to modify the character of the light passing through the lens to the sensitive film. Its effectiveness depends upon three factors:

1. The color of the light reflected from the object (which of course depends somewhat on the color of the incident light).

2. The color transmission of the filter (usually termed, oppositely, *absorption*).

3. The color sensitivity of the negative emulsion.

The use of a filter therefore alters the gray values of the image in relation to the colors of the subject, increases or decreases the "contrast" in the image, and (in landscape work) increases or diminishes atmospheric-haze effects.

To understand thoroughly the practical application of filters, you must first become acquainted with the effects obtained on film without the use of filters. From this point of departure you can explore the potent fields of control that filters make possible for you.

Consider an ideal subject—a landscape containing white rocks, green trees, a red barn, and blue sky. If you make a photograph on old-fashioned color-blind blue-sensitive film,* you see that in the final print the sky is very light, the rocks are fairly light, but not quite so brilliant as you might suppose, and the green trees and the barn are very dark. The film, being sensitive only to blue light, does not respond to the other components of white light reflected from the rock, but is fully responsive to all the blue light contained in the sky and reflected from the other objects. As the sky is dominantly blue, it is easy to understand why

---

* This is used nowadays principally for copying and engraving, and is known simply as "commercial" film. It has certain expressive uses; see Book 2, p. 5.

it should appear very light in the print. The image of the trees on this blue-sensitive film is limited to the amount of bluish light reflected from the foliage. While the proportionate amount of blue light from foliage may be fairly high, the *total* amount of light reflected from the foliage may be comparatively small (as foliage is usually of fairly low brightness), and the image of the trees is therefore certain to be very deep in tone, if not practically black. The same applies to the semisaturated red of the barn.

Two other factors alter the values of reflected light. One is the highlights, or specular reflections of sunlight, which are practically pure white light and of great relative brightness. The second is the shadow cast by the small units of subject structure that are perceived as such only on very close inspection; at a distance these small shadows merely serve to degrade the average brightness. However, as the shadows in landscape are illuminated chiefly with blue light from the sky, the use of a blue-sensitive film will, to a certain extent, proportionately elevate the shadow values. (Any panchromatic or orthochromatic emulsion can be rendered color-blind—that is, sensitive only to blue light—by using a sharp-cut filter, which absorbs all colors but blue.)

An *orthochromatic* emulsion is sensitive to both blue and green light, but is quite blind to red light, though its sensitivity approaches the orange band of the spectrum. The same landscape mentioned above, rendered with an orthochromatic film, appears somewhat as follows: The sky is light, but not so light as with the color-blind film, because the response to blue light is proportionately less (in relation to the total sensitivity of the emulsion). On the other hand, the green trees are considerably elevated in value, and the white rocks also appear lighter than they did with the blue-sensitive film, because the film is responding to green as well as to blue elements of the white light reflected from the rocks. In proportion to the other values the shadows are a bit deeper; being illuminated largely by blue light, they drop in value in the same proportion as the blue sky. The "red" barn is recorded in proportion to the blue, yellow, and green components in its color. The effects of an orthochromatic film can be achieved with panchromatic film by use of "minus-red" filters, such as Wratten filters Nos. 38, 38A, and 66. A short description of these filters follows:

FOR ORTHOCHROMATIC EFFECTS WITH PANCHROMATIC FILM

	Transmission in				Approx.
Filter No.	Blue	Green	Red	Total	Factor
38	70%	50%	12%	42%	2 or 2.5
38A	55	25	1	16	6
66	35	75	20	58	2

It is obvious that considerable control is possible by using the above filters. Perhaps No. 66 will give the most satisfactory results, in view of its high green transmission and small exposure factor.*

Now if you expose with a *panchromatic* emulsion—that is, a film sensitive to all colors—your landscape appears very much as follows: The sky is definitely deeper in tone, the blue components now being but a fractional part of the total light to which the film is sensitive. The greens will not appear as light as they did in the orthochromatic film, for they too are but part of the total spectrum to

---

* See *Kodak Wratten Light Filters* and other publications of the Eastman Kodak Company.

which the film is balanced. The red barn is rendered fairly light and the white rocks have an increased brilliancy over the orthochromatic rendering, since all the colors comprising white light are now recorded upon the film.

"Panchromatic" is a generalized term for emulsions sensitive to all visible colors, but there are numerous varieties of panchromatic film with slightly different properties of color sensitivity. For instance, Type C Panchromatic Film is highly sensitive to red light and therefore its use is indicated when short exposures are required with tungsten light, which has a much higher proportion of red than has daylight. Type B Panchromatic Film has a slightly higher sensitivity to green light and slightly less sensitivity to red light. Consequently it is fine for general landscape work and is indicated in portraiture when undue emphasis on red lips is not desired.

Filter Types and Designations

In the simplest terms, a filter transmits light of its own color, and absorbs (in varying degree) other colors. The actual transmission-absorption capacities of a filter cannot be accurately judged by the eye. Some idea can be gained by a cursory glance at the transmission charts and tables in the book *Wratten Light Filters*. Literally hundreds of specific filters are available, but the practicing photographer need use only a few basic types in general work.

In these books, I prefer to mention only the Wratten series of filters; they are standard in this country. Other makes are available and entirely satisfactory, and their relationship to similar types in the Wratten series can be determined.

In Book 1 (p. 104) there is a table of filters in common use. With the exception of the Wratten No. 12 (minus-blue), the practicing photographer will seldom need other filters than those listed. In the first edition of Book 1 (p. 106) the Color Compensating CC series is listed; these are now known as "light-balancing filters," Series 81 and 82. For students inclined to more detailed study of filters and their physical effects, I warmly recommend *Kodak Wratten Light Filters*, published by the Eastman Kodak Company. Another Kodak publication, *Kodak Filters and Pola-Screens*, is a simpler, but nevertheless inclusive, popular text on filters, their types, sizes, and applications. In view of the easy availability of these books it is not necessary to give complete listings here. Therefore I concentrate on the application of certain filters to the problem of photography in natural light, and list only a few basic types.

For all ordinary purposes filters mounted in "B" glass suffice. But for precise work or work with long-focus lenses, best results are assured with filters in sheet-gelatin form, which can be used before or behind the lens, or placed between the components of the lens. These sheets of dyed gelatin are so thin that they show no appreciable refraction effects. They are now treated with lacquer, which minimizes damage from finger marks and abrasion.

---

* Designations of other makes of filters are often confusing in relation to the standard Wratten designations. For example, the Zeiss-Ikon G-1, G-2, G-3, and G-4 roughly comprise the Wratten filters K-1, K-2, K-3, and G, and the Zeiss-Ikon B-2 (light bluish filter) has nothing to do with the Wratten B (monochromatic green filter). *All* filters mentioned in this book are those of the Wratten Series. Polarizers are made of Polaroid (manufactured by the Polaroid Corporation, Cambridge, Mass.).

Filters can be classified in several ways; sometimes the classifications overlap. In practical work, the following groupings should, I believe, suffice:

Under standard daylight (or standard tungsten) illumination, a given film has a certain response to the spectrum. This response may be "photometrically accurate" but not visually satisfying; that is, it may render unlike colors in gray values so similar as to suggest little differentiation. However, you can alter black-and-white values for satisfying expressive results by using an appropriate filter. Examples of correction filters are:

> K2, used with Type B Panchromatic Film in daylight
>
> X1, used with Type C Panchromatic Film in daylight (or with Type B Panchromatic Film in tungsten light).
>
> X2, used with Type C Panchromatic Film in Tungsten Light.
>
> K1, and the Aero filters are also used in the mild "correction" classification.

Contrast Filters

"Contrast" in relation to the photographic print is both physical and psychological. Mere *differences* of value may not adequately describe expressive contrast effects. But in the common meaning of "contrast," you will find that certain filters—under certain conditions of illumination and subject value—produce images of increased contrast or separation of tone. Actually, you can render one or more colors of the subject in lighter or darker values of gray in the print. This control is achieved through exposure and developmental procedures, application of the proper filter, and by control in the printing procedures. Some "contrast" filters are:

> No. 12   (minus-blue). Absorbs blue light; transmits other colors.
>
> No. 15 (G). Absorbs all blue light and some green; (stronger than No. 12).
>
> No. 23 (E). Absorbs blue and some green and transmits orange and red light.
>
> No. 25 (A). Absorbs blue and most green light and transmits red light. (monochromatic filter).
>
> No. 58 (B). Absorbs most blue and red light and transmits green light. (monochromatic filter).
>
> No. 47 (C5). Absorbs most red light and most green light, and transmits blue light, (monochromatic filter).

The filters, F, N, and C4 are related to A, B, and C5, but are even more selective, transmitting only their own color with scarcely any overlap. They are referred to as "sharp-cut" monochromatic filters, while the A, B, and C5 are called "broadcut" filters.

However, desirable contrast effects can also be produced with mild correction filters, together with certain exposure and developmental procedures. Whereas a red filter gives contrast by darkening both blue and green, a K2 darkens only the blue. By following the usual procedure for increased contrast (reduced exposure and increased development), and using a K2 (or other mild correction filter) you can obtain relatively high contrast without distortion of color values other than the blues, which are darkened.

If you combine two filters—say a K2 and a G—you get only the effect of the strongest filter. In practical work, combining two or more filters is not advised.

Photometric Filters

These are designed to modify light to specific measurable quality. Though only occasionally used in practical black-and-white photography, they are important in color photography, where the quality of the light must be adjusted to the color response of the film.

Ultraviolet and Extreme Violet Absorption Filters

True ultraviolet light is absorbed by glass, but transmitted by quartz filters. The Wratten Skylight and Haze filters absorb extreme violet and violet light, and when used with black-and-white film, slightly reduce atmospheric haze and deepen the values of shadows illuminated by skylight. These, and the Wratten Light-Balancing filters are essential with color film, especially under overcast skies or in full shade, and at high altitudes.

Polarizer

This device, being used more and more, offers certain controls heretofore impossible. The important effects of the polarizer are:

1. To darken the sky (maximum darkening at 90° from the sun)

2. To remove reflections from nonspecular surfaces (maximum 36° from the surface; 54° from normal)

3. To reduce distant atmospheric haze (if within polarizing angle)

The above effects are achieved without altering the relative color values of the subject; but the polarizer can also be used with color filters if desired. (See page 32 for further data on polarizers.)

Summary

Throughout this book, emphasis is on minimizing the use of filters; their application is recommended for achieving desired interpretative effects.

We are accustomed to thinking of reds and yellows as "warm" colors. These, however, are given off by incandescent objects at relatively low temperatures, the color of the radiated light progressing from dark to lighter red and then throughout increasingly lighter shades to blue as the temperature continues to increase. It is therefore difficult to reconcile the term "warm" (reddish) light with low color temperature (see page 1). It may help to remove the confusion to recapitulate the facts on color and light:

1. The sun gives warmer (redder) light early and late in the day; the color temperature is then lower.

2. A clear blue sky gives colder (bluer) light than a hazy or partially cloudy sky in which the haze or clouds are reflecting sunlight; the color temperature of the clear sky is higher.

3. The light on an overcast day is cold (blue); it is of higher color temperature than light from sun and clear sky.

4. Shadows illuminated by open sky are colder (bluer) when the sky is clear than when it is misty or partially cloudy; shadows are of higher color temperature under a clear sky than under a misty one.

5. At sunset, the direct sunlight may be very warm (reddish) and the light from the sky overhead very cold (blue); the color temperature of the sky overhead is higher than that of the western horizon.

6. Light reflected from brilliant sunset clouds is very warm; it is of low color temperature.

In color photography these effects are quite pronounced, and may give exaggerated results unless controlled somewhat by the use of proper light-balancing filters (formerly referred to as color compensators). In black-and-white photography they influence the degree of contrast obtained in the final image. For example:

1. At high altitudes (deeper skies) shadows are colder, and blue-absorbing filters render them darker than usual (unless a higher exposure factor is used).

2. Objects illuminated by direct sun very early or late in the day are rendered darker than usual on orthochromatic film (not senstive to red). If a yellow or red filter is used with panchromatic film these objects are rendered lighter than usual in relation to other colors (which are darkened by the film) unless a reduced exposure factor is used. At sunrise or sunset the sky may be suffused with the same warm color that appears on clouds, mountains, buildings, etc., and it is obviously difficult, if not futile, to attempt "separations" by the use of filters. Only expanded contrast can augment the impression of brilliancy and tonal variation. (See Figure 14.)

15. Oak Tree, Noon, California. A good example of blue-filter application. The original print carries the mood of blazing noon light; detail is retained in the trunk of the tree. A similar picture was made without filter but with increased exposure and reduced development; the sky is not as white, and the foliage is lighter in tone.

Because a filter absorbs some of the colors of the light directed toward it, the total amount of light it transmits to the film is less than if it were not employed. The effective transmission of the filter depends not only on its own characteristics, but also on the color balance of the incident light and the color of the subject. The determination of the exposure factor of a given filter for a given film is based on the color sensitivity of the film and on standard illumination (daylight or tungsten) of a neutral-gray scale; the manufacturer indicates on his instruction sheets just what this ideal exposure factor is—that is, by how much the exposure must be increased with a given filter to render the image of a gray card in the same density that would be obtained without the filter. For example, a K2 filter requires twice the normal exposure with panchromatic film and three times the normal exposure with orthochromatic film. The orthochromatic film requires more exposure chiefly because it is not sensitive to the red light transmitted by the filter. Now if the light is warmer than normal (that is, more yellowish), the exposure factor will be smaller; if the light is colder than normal (that is, more bluish), the exposure factor will be greater.

An A (red) filter may have a factor of 8 with panchromatic film; with ortho-chromatic film it may require 1000 times normal exposure, simply because the film is not sensitive to red, and what effective light is transmitted represents slight "leaks" in the filter-absorption curve.

A C5 filter (blue) may have an exposure factor of 6 with panchromatic film, and of 4 with orthochromatic film (because of the higher sensitivity of the latter film to blue light). On clear days, when light and shadows are quite blue, the exposure factor is less; early and late in the day it is more for objects directly illuminated by the warm-toned sunlight and less for objects directly illuminated by the open sky.

A good general rule of thumb can be expressed as follows:

1. With filters transmitting "warmer" light:
   a. *Decrease* the exposure factor with early or late sunlight, or with subjects of definite "warm" color values.
   b. *Increase* the exposure factor at high altitudes, under clear blue skies, and under overcast, and with subjects of definitely "cold" color values.

2. With filters transmitting "colder" light:
   a. *Increase* the exposure factor with early or late sunlight, or with subjects of definite warm color values.
   b. *Decrease* the exposure factor at high altitudes, under clear blue skies, and under overcast, and with subjects of definite "cold" color values.

The Effects of Filters

We have seen how each of three film types responds to a given landscape (page 21). Let us see how filters can be used to modify the effects with *blue-sensitive (color blind)* film. The only filter that would have any appreciable contrast effect is a "haze" filter that would minimize the extreme violet, and thereby *slightly* reduce the sky and distant shadow values. Its exposure factor would be very slight—in fact, it could be disregarded.

A blue filter (C5) would but slightly alter the basic values of the subject, but would accentuate the atmospheric effect. Its exposure factor could be very low, perhaps only 2x.

With *orthochromatic film* the following filters could be used:

C5 (blue). Further lightens the sky and accentuates the atmospheric effects.

K1 and **K2** (yellow). Slightly darken the sky and the shadows and lighten the foliage and the barn.

G (orange). Further darkens the sky, and lightens yellow-green foliage, and to a greater extent than with the K2, would lighten the barn.

No. 12 (minus-blue). This would perhaps be better to use than the G, because it would have the same effect on the sky, would transmit a little more green but with a slightly lower exposure factor.

With *panchromatic film*, the following filters could be used:

K1 and **K2.** Slightly darken the sky and the shadows, lighten the foliage and the barn.

No. 12 and **G.** Like K1 and K2, except to a greater degree. The rock would be rendered quite light.

X1 and **B.** Darken the sky and the barn and the shadows, but lighten yellow-green foliage. The rock would be slightly reduced in value.

A (red). Darkens the sky considerably, darkens the diffuse reflections from the foliage (but not the specular reflection from the leaves), and renders the barn quite light. The rock would be fairly light. A general impression of "contrast" would result, largely because of the general darkening of the sky and the shadows, and also because of the deep penetration of the red rays through the emulsion (see page 21).

C5. Lightens the sky, darkens foliage and barn, and accentuates atmospheric effects.

With all film, the polarizer gives darkened skies, and reduces reflections (assuming the optical axis is at proper angles to the subject). The effects of lens and camera flare on negative contrast must not be overlooked (see Book 2, p. 53), and of course contrast control can be achieved by variations in exposure and development, as described in Book 2.

Each photographer is urged to make experiments with various subjects in his particular environment. To repeat, in high altitudes or in very clear desert regions of the country, the skies are much bluer than at sea level or in industrial areas. Not only does the sky appear deeper in tone, but shadow values are more intense. Overfiltering must be guarded against, otherwise a typical "lunar" aspect is certain to result. In a normal city on the eastern American seaboard, the published filter factors are reasonably applicable. In highly industrialized areas, where vast amounts of smoke and haze are a constant feature of the scene, the factors of all filters except the bluish filters can be appreciably reduced, as daylight is "warmer" than normal, owing to a yellowish haze in the air. As the clarity of the scene increases and the color of the light becomes "colder," higher filter factors are required for the yellow, green, and red filters and lower factors for the bluish filters.

Shadows are complex. Too many assume that they are illuminated only with blue light from the sky. This is true with most large outdoor subjects, but not for small shadows existing in environments of a dominant color. For instance, a pine tree standing in a yellow-green meadow; the eye, with its rather inclusive psychological adjustments, perceives little difference of color in various parts of the shadows of this pine tree. A color photograph, however, would show that the shadows at the bottom of the tree trunk definitely suggest the colors of the surrounding meadow, and that as the eye passes upward the sky color predominates. This is perfectly obvious in a color photograph, but what relationship does this observation have to black-and-white photography? It is simply this: With an unfiltered panchromatic film the difference in values would be slight, as this film has relatively low sensitivity to green light, and would render the shadows near the base of the tree about the same as the upper shadows illuminated from the open sky. Apply an ordinary K2 filter; now the shadows at the base of the tree are somewhat brighter, because of the yellow-green light reflected from the grass, but the shadows of the upper part of the tree are quite noticeably deepened in tone because the yellow filter absorbs so much of the blue light reflected from the sky. The maximum difference in value results from the use of a yellow-green filter transmitting approximately the same color as that of the meadow. The bottom shadows are then rendered in the highest possible tonalities, in relation to these brightnesses, but the upper shadows are definitely darkened in tone. The use of a red filter renders the upper shadows very dark, but has less effect than the yellow-green filter on the shadows at the base of the tree. A blue filter has just the opposite effect; the shadows at the bottom of the tree probably appear a little deeper than the shadows at the top of the tree. But it must be remembered that the foregoing is merely a theoretical discussion. Variations in the basic color and brightness of the tree trunk and in the brightness and color of meadow and sky would profoundly alter the photographic effects. In high altitudes, or wherever clear blue skies and brilliant sunlight prevail, the relationships between shadows and high values are always extreme. The great danger in ordinary practice is that extreme deepening of the shadows may destroy the impression of light.

If the filter used to gain certain desired sky effects makes shadows too dark, shadow values can be built up by pre-exposing the film by a given amount (see Book 2, p. 109, and page 114 of this book). In color photography the colors and values of shadows can be modified by pre-exposure to cards of appropriate colors.

A word of caution here. Throughout these *Basic Photo* books, as I have often explained, my readers have concentrated on discussion of normal conditions and normal effects so as to establish a firm foundation from which we can, at will, make "departures from reality" and acquire adequate techniques for our expressive needs. I would not want anyone to think I would state that a sky could not be black (see Fig. 1), or that skin should not be rendered completely white, or that the shadows in an architectural photograph should not be unrealistically deep in tone. There is great magic in experimental and expressive photography, and the artist is not to be bound by "normal" rules and regulations. Nature is tremendously rich and complex, and the imagination is capable of infinite variety; all we can do here is to suggest logical procedures that will open the way to great experiences in photography.

16. Old Wood and Wire. Photographs of this character depend upon precision and brilliancy for their effect. In the original print the space between the boards and the back of the knothole is completely black (Zone 0). Shadows on the wood itself are chiefly of Zone I value. The high values were on about Zone VI of the brightness scale, but were elevated to Zone VIII by expansion in development. The print is "on the edge" of being harsh; if the impression of brilliancy were further forced, only bleak *contrast* would remain. Textural studies of wood, rock, etc. must have an all-over sharpness and clarity; witness Edward Weston's revealing images of rock, shell, and wood; Paul Strand's pictures of New England and Mexico, in which substances vibrate and glow with a super-reality of tone and texture. Such photographs depend upon more than mere optical sharpness—but clarity is the prime physical quality.

Great confusion persists with regard to the meaning of the terms "texture" and "pattern." *Pattern* simply refers to an orderly spatial disposition of forms (in nature or in the print), whereas *texture* is a property of the surface substance. It can be emphasized or subordinated by light. We can say that a rough stone wall shows a lot of *detail;* any good lens can render a sharp image of this detail (and we should speak of the *good delineation* by the lens). Detail rounded out by appropriate tonal values is revealed as *texture.* Texture is both a tactile and a visual quality; that is to say, it is three-dimensional. One cannot feel detail with the fingers, but texture is appreciated by both touch and vision; so let us say that a rough stone wall possesses texture, and that the photograph of the stone wall should reveal this texture in a more or less exaggerated way.

If a photograph conveys the conviction of texture, it will usually convey the impression of substance and light. By analyzing textured surfaces we find proof that texture is a three-dimensional quality—under a powerful microscope, what appears to be a smooth polished surface becomes an intricate organization of heights and hollows possessing highlights, shadows, and an infinite variety of forms and values. Such an object ordinarily seems smooth and of continuous tone because its surface textures, due to their minuteness in relation to our size, fall below the limits of visual resolution, so that we no longer sense three dimensions in the surface. For the same reason a highly textured object at a great distance will appear smooth and of continuous tone.

Thus in visualizing substances in photographic terms you must consider whether or not the textures seen with your eyes can be resolved in the photographic image. You may visualize an interesting photographic composition of textures only to find that in the final print the rich textural surfaces of the subject appear as continuous, and perhaps uninteresting, grays. A very practical example of how to use these principles lies in photographing someone with a poor complexion. A large head may show skin defects to a distressing degree and the slightest underexposure exaggerates them; but if the subject is pictured at a greater distance, so that the image of the head is smaller, there is more emphasis on the structure of the face and textural qualities are minimized.

Consider photographing rocky landscapes, another instance that presents serious problems in textural rendition. Beyond a certain distance, a great field of granite boulders will appear as perfectly smooth stones, the natural textures being beyond the resolving power of the lens and/or the emulsion. In order to suggest the substance of these stones it is necessary to include in the very near foreground a boulder in which the texture is adequately revealed. You can then say that the photograph "reads well." While you cannot see the textures in the distant boulders, you *can* see it in the near boulder, and you assume that all the boulders are of the same material. It is this *awareness of substance* that is of vital importance in any interpretive photography. The photograph, no matter what its function may be, must "read" clearly.

The impression of light in a print profoundly influences the impression of texture. Any textured object photographed with a large proportion of shadow is difficult to understand if the shadow is rendered completely black. If the greater part of the image is of well-illuminated surfaces, the mind can perhaps automatically visualize the substance of small shadow areas.

THE POLARIZERS

In recent years the widespread application of Polaroid (the proprietary name for the polarizing material manufactured by the Polaroid Corporation, Cambridge, Mass.)* has had an important effect on photography. Apart from its effectiveness in reducing reflections from a great variety of surfaces, it can be used to deepen the value of the sky (at certain angles to the sun) and to clarify distant landscapes—both being accomplished without altering the intrinsic color values of the subject. It provides the only known way of directly darkening blue skies in color photography. The principles of the polarization of light can be found in any physics textbook; the photographer need not know these in order to use the polarizer, because the effect of the polarizer—for all practical purposes—can be visually checked before exposing the negative. In addition, the polarizers as manufactured for standard cameras are orientated in a mount that indicates the proper positioning for maximum effect on the sky. The effect on other subjects can be determined by direct viewing through the polarizer, then placing the screen over the lens in the selected position, or by viewing on the ground glass. The polarizer can be used with color filters if desired. The basic exposure factor for the polarizer is $2\frac{1}{2}$x; the exposure factors for other filters used with it must be *multiplied* by, not added to, the factor. For example, if the basic exposure was $\frac{1}{10}$ second, the use of a polarizer and a K2 filter would demand an exposure of $\frac{1}{2}$ second ($\frac{1}{10}$x$2\frac{1}{2}$x2).

The exposure factor of $2\frac{1}{2}$x applies to the transmission of unpolarized light; that is, the part of the subject which is not polarized will require $2\frac{1}{2}$x exposure with the polarizer to match the density obtained without the screen. All polarized areas are rendered as having *less* density in the negative, depending on the degree of polarization. But, as mentioned above, the degree of polarization can be *visually* appraised, and the effect will be closely matched on the photographic film.

Effect of Polarizer on the Sky

As light from the blue sky is polarized, the polarizer will give a marked depth of tone to the sky at the optimum angle from the sun (90°). This deepening of the sky becomes less as the angle from the sun increases or decreases. Therefore the use of a wide-angle lens on subjects containing much sky area will produce a definite change of sky value across the image—deepest at the optimum angle to the sun, and lighter on either side of this limited sky area. Hence the most consistent effect is obtained with lenses of long focal length. When the blue sky is polarized, clouds and haze are exaggerated in contrast against the sky, and the sky itself is given more "shape" and tonal intensity. Frequently a hazy "opaque" sky (especially near the horizon) will not respond to ordinary color filters but will be effectively deepened in value by the polarizer.

As with color filters, the lowering of sky values may produce a merging of tone with the surfaces of other elements of the scene. This effect can be largely anticipated by visual examination of the scene through the polarizer, but for a more precise evaluation I suggest a Wratten No. 90 viewing filter be used with

---

*Available as Polaroid filters and Kodak Pola-Screens.

the polarizer to minimize the color contrasts of the scene to the eye. Do NOT use the No. 90 filter on the camera! As mentioned before, color filters can be used with the polarizer and a wide variety of tonal effects obtained.

Effects of Polarizer on Distant Haze

Not only the sky itself is subject to control by the polarizer, but atmospheric haze is subject to it to a certain extent—the greater the distance, the more obvious the effect. The amount of polarization can be controlled by visual examination through the polarizer; the character of the intervening haze and the sometimes complex illumination from open sky and/or clouds does not permit a consistent orientation of the screen, as it does with the sky alone. Clarification of haze can be augmented by the use of regular color filters. The polarizer can be used to good advantage with a strong color filter in telephotography, but it is obvious that the optical quality of the screen must be adequate; otherwise definition will be impaired.

Effects of Polarizer on Water

Distant bodies of water, such as the sea or lakes, can be definitely lowered in tone by the polarizer. Unless the surfaces are very smooth, the reflections of the sky will be broken and diffuse, and the polarizing effect only partial. If the surfaces are smooth and unruffled, the polarizer will lower the values to a striking degree. The various bands of color and values often observed on the ocean will be greatly exaggerated by use of the polarizer. Reflections of distant clouds and mountains, and the sheen of the sun itself, can be modified by the device, but extremely intense reflections can never be completely removed.

Near surfaces of water respond to the polarizer with most interesting effects. Still water may have sky and environmental reflections almost entirely removed, revealing details at the bottom of pools and streams that it would otherwise be impossible to photograph. However, in our enthusiasm for the spectacular controls of the polarizer we must not forget the esthetic dangers that lie in its misuse. If you are photographing a pool, for example, and you remove *all* the surface reflections, you no longer have the *substance of the pool!* Fortunately, the degree of polarization can be visually adjusted to just the right amount—and this is dictated by both practical and esthetic requirements. Just as the *presence* of still water is revealed by its reflections, so is the quality of foam and dashing water largely defined by the sparkles of reflected sunlight in the myriad droplets and particles of spray. The polarizer can reduce these effects, and cautious use with such subjects is advisable.

Wet streets, roofs, rocks, etc. are subject to control by the polarizer (assuming the angles of reflection are right), but again you must be alert not to remove reflections essential to the interpretation of the subject.

Ice and snow give up their glitter and sparkle to the polarizer, and it is of the greatest importance that this loss be anticipated when using the polarizers in winter-landscape photography. In winter close-ups—snow details, icicles, etc.— we are sometimes confronted with a bewildering complex of reflections that can confuse our compositions. Sometimes the polarizer will work miracles by reducing the reflections to just the right degree.

Effects of Polarizer on Various Reflecting Surfaces

The optimum polarizing angle from surfaces of water, glass, polished wood, painted surfaces, etc. is 34°. When the axis of the lens (as well as that of the polarizing filter) is at this angle to the subject, the maximum polarizing effect obtains. The reflections from many metallic surfaces are not polarized, and the polarizer has no effect on these reflections. But any polarizing effect is always visible to the eye (through the polarizer); hence no question can exist as to the effect of the device on various surfaces.

The applications of the polarizer must now be obvious, but you must always be on guard to prevent misinterpretation of substance. It is of unquestioned advantage to be able to photograph through a store window and record the display within minus the confusion of a myriad unrelated reflections. But it is quite another thing to photograph a bright and shiny automobile or a fine piece of glazed ceramic and find that you have eliminated an essential quality of the objects—their sparkling reflectivity.

The polarizer is helpful in portraiture; reflections from glasses can be reduced, and unwanted reflections from oily or perspiring skin can be removed. But do not remove the important catchlights from the eyes!

Surfaces of polished wood can be controlled so as to reveal the grain of the material; structural details of leather and fabrics can be strengthened; glare from roadways and roofs can be reduced. The uses of this device are many indeed; it is advisable to have it on hand always, both in the field and in the studio.

Perhaps this basic rule should always be evoked when using a polarizer: **Reduce or eliminate surface reflections only when it is of greater esthetic and practical importance to reveal what the reflections obscure.**

17a. River, Mountains, Sky: K1 filter.   **17b. Same;** K1 filter and Polarizer.

18. Redwood Snag, near Scotia, California. Made with a 5⅜-inch lens on a 5x7 negative. Expanded contrast.

VISUALIZATION

A technique difficult for any photographer to master is the visualization of various colors in terms of black-and-white tonalities. The response of various emulsions to different colors of light can be accurately measured only if all the colors are considered as saturated and emanating from surfaces of equal reflective intensity. When the reflective intensities of the surface vary and when the colors are of different degrees of saturation, much confusion results. The classic example is the red apple on the green leaf; the panchromatic film records both these values in the *same shade of gray*. It may not be emotionally or even representationally adequate. This does not concern the photometricist, but it profoundly concerns the practical photographer. His problem is to obtain an image that is an adequate visual and/or emotional statement. He may visualize certain tones in the print that are not photometrically accurate.

The conventional term "correction" as applied to the use of filters has little practical or expressive meaning. "Corrected to what?" is the first question raised by the creative photographer. The scientist will reply that the use of filters "corrects" the image in terms of the photometric equivalence of monotones. On the other hand, the photographer may desire an image in which the grays are *not* the accepted photometric equivalents of given colors. He may say that it is a corrective procedure (from his creative point of view) if—by using the filters that produced the desired effect—he has achieved an image of the red apple on the green leaf that is both emotionally and visually acceptable.

When an emotional or an esthetic departure from reality is concerned, we must recognize that the control is so highly personalized that an experimental approach is imperative. Values and colors should be *first* recognized as they actually are in relation to monotone values, rather than for their emotional qualities. If you study the world about you through a monochromatic viewing filter (such as the Wratten No. 90) in which all colors are reduced to their approximate related monochromatic value, you will quickly grasp what is meant by the foregoing. You will instantly see how several colors that to the eye have a beautiful clarity and separation will appear in monochrome as almost identical grays. When subjects of such color relationships are noted, you should then experiment, making exposures with various filters, and noting how the relative values can be changed. Interpretation is based on the intentional modulation of factual values. But the ability actually to obtain these tones in the image, through use of filters and control of exposure and development, is the mark of an artist who has mastered his medium.

In theory, a red filter should render green grass black in the photographic image, and this would be absolutely true if the grass were entirely green—and if it reflected only diffused light. But such is not the case. Green grass reflects a definite amount of white light along with its dominating green color, and this white light is composed of all colors, including red, and the red component is freely transmitted by the red filter. The green grass will be definitely deepened in tone, but not rendered black. In addition, every blade of grass shows a certain amount of specular reflection—call it "highlights"—and the shine and sparkle are especially apparent under direct sunlight. These highlights are of course very bright (being direct reflections of the light source), so that no matter what filter is used, they are rendered very light in the image. Hence with panchromatic film and a red filter (or with color-blind film and no filter) grass can be rendered with both delicacy and depth of tone; in either case the surfaces reflecting diffuse light are rendered quite dark, but the specular reflections come through very light.

In any event, the progression from visualization to the desired image should first be based on the scene as photographed on a panchromatic film *without* filters. This gives you a point of departure, and the approach to the visualization should then be made through application of the mildest correction filters (that is, the K1, K2, etc.), and not by daring experiments with "contrast" filters.

The blind faith that the use of filters will overcome all photographic obstacles must be supplanted with the facts. In Figure 19 a-f we see a typical mountain landscape photographed without filter and with 5 common filters. The limitations of the reproduction process prevent study of the subtle differences in the original image, but there is not as much difference in the six images as one might casually imagine would obtain from the use of such varied filters. With the exception of the red and blue filters, the effects of the filters are surprisingly similar. The reason the filters do not achieve a profound modification of values with subjects of this character is that all parts of the scene have a low saturation of color; that is, everything is reflecting a high percentage of white light along with its dominant color. On the other hand, in Figure 21 you have a photograph of a color chart produced with inks of high saturation. Note the extraordinary alteration of values with the different filters.

If you are photographing a typical landscape of rocks, trees, and a sky in which very delicate clouds exist your first impulse might be to apply a red filter "to bring out the clouds." You should first ask yourself what the *mood* of the scene is, and what you wish the resultant mood of the print to be. If the clouds are delicate, the application of a powerful red filter would simply darken the sky and the shadows, creating a high-contrast effect that may not in any way relate to the desired mood. Considering a K1 filter as possibly inadequate, you might then think of a K2, which would, in view of your experience, seem about right, or a "minus-blue" (Wratten No. 12) filter, which for many purposes gives the optimum effect out of doors. Use of a G (or orange-yellow) filter might produce too harsh an effect. Now, assuming that a K2 filter is appropriate to your cloud-sky problem, you must then review the other elements of the scene, because the photographer often thinks only of the dominant elements and disregards others, frequently with unfortunate results. As the landscape may contain numerous large forms close at hand (rocks, for example) that cast rather strong shadows of considerable size, the K2 filter might very well cause these shadows to be rendered so dark as to destroy the desired mood; that is, a mood of enveloping and delicate light. With this second effect recognized, about the only practical solution would be to use a K1 filter with slightly reduced exposure (being certain that the shadows are placed not lower than Zone III), or to retain the K2 filter and slightly increase the exposure, followed by slightly lessened development.

Another factor in the scene relates to the green foliage. The visualization of the values of this foliage in the print suggests use of a broad-cut green filter such as the X1, which, while having approximately the same effect as the K2 filter on sky and shadow values, lightens the foliage values, thereby intensifying the mood of enveloping delicate light. The B (monochromatic green) filter would render the foliage quite light, but would also distort the red and blue objects.

19a. Landscape. No filter.

19b. With C5 (blue) filter.

19c. With K2 (yellow) filter.

19d. With X1 (green) filter.

19e. With G (yellow-orange) filter.

19f. With A (red) filter.

38

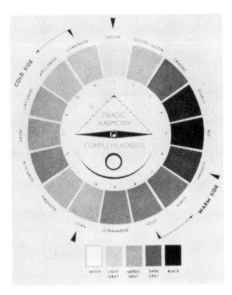

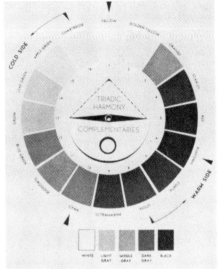

20a. No filter.

20b. With K2 (yellow) filter.

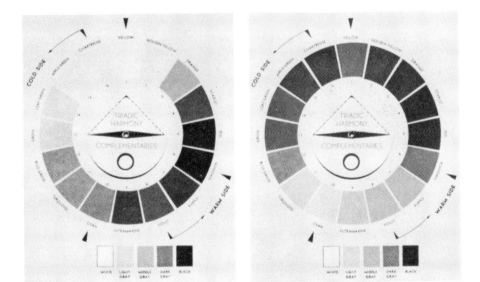

20c. With G (yellow-orange) filter.

20d. With C5 (blue) filter.

20a-d. Hiler Color Chart (courtesy Hilaire Hiler, Fremont College, Santa Fe, N. M.) photographed without filter and with Wratten K2, G, and C5 filters, on *Verichrome* (orthochromatic) film.

There is considerable popular confusion about filters, their transmission characteristics, and their exposure (multiplying) factors. Perhaps this will be partially clarified by study of the table, p. 41 (for a few of the most-used filters). The source for this data is *Kodak Wratten Light Filters*, published by the Eastman Kodak Company. Refer also to the table on page 22.

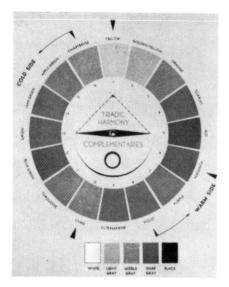

21a. No filter.

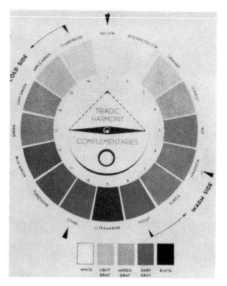

21b. With K2 (yellow) filter.

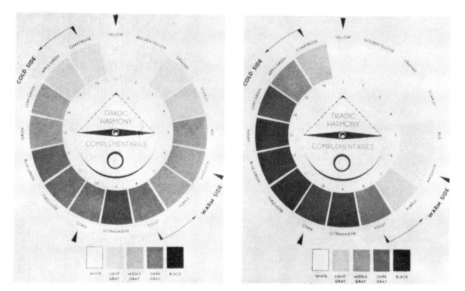

21c. With No. 12 (minus-blue) filter.

21d. With A (red) filter.

21a-f. Hiler Color Chart photographed without filter and with Wratten K2, No. 12, A, B2, and C5 filters on *Panchromatic* film.

At first glance the reader may be perplexed to note that none of the filters transmit more than 90% of the incident light; how, then, we may ask, are certain colors rendered *lighter* in the photograph than when no filter is used? For example, transmission of the K2 filter in the yellow regions of the spectrum (600mμ) is about 88%, and yet a yellow object will appear

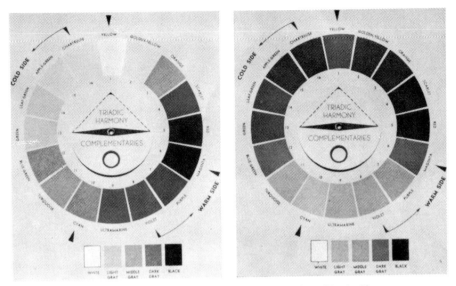

21e. With B2 (green) filter. **21f. With C5 (blue) filter.**

lighter than when no filter is before the lens. The total transmission of light (from 400 mμ to 700mμ) of the K2 filter is 77.5%. A multiplying factor of 2x is recommended for panchromatic film with daylight, and 1.5x for the same film and tungsten light. The total transmission percentage is *not* a positive indication of the exposure factor, because characteristics of the light and of the sensitive materials vary considerably. If the K2 filter transmits 88% yellow light and a multiplying factor of 2x is applied to the exposure time, it is obvious that about 176% of yellow light is transmitted to the film in comparison to the amount of yellow light transmitted without filter. This same filter transmits about 58% of blue-green; with the 2x factor, the relative transmitted value would be 116%. The filter transmits very little blue—say only about 1% of wavelength 455mμ. Hence if the lens transmits all colors equally:

Blue	Blue-green	Yellow	Red
100%	100%	100%	100%

The transmission of the K2 filter will be approximately:

Blue	Blue-green	Yellow	Red
2%	116%	176%	180%

The actual photographic effect depends, as we have said, upon light and film characteristics; a red filter, for example, would have no effect upon an orthochromatic film.

However, the transmission values as listed below will suggest, roughly, the relative lightening and darkening of various colors of the spectrum that will obtain with the filters. In actual practice (as discussed on pages 17 et. seq.) we seldom find pure colors in nature; a red rock will not respond to a red filter as will a definitely red band of the spectrum or some pigment or dye of high color saturation.

Filter	K1	K2	No. 12	G	A	B2	C5
TRANSMISSION of the following colors: (approximate wavelengths)							
400mμ Violet	8.0	—	—	—	—	—	6.0
450mμ Blue (deep)	29.4	—	—	—	—	—	49.0
500mμ Blue-green	83.2	58.8	2.5	—	—	17.4	9.9
550mμ Green	88.4	85.4	84.0	81.5	—	39.8	—
600mμ Yellow	89.2	88.2	89.2	88.2	54.8	2.4	—
650mμ Orange	89.7	89.7	90.0	90.0	87.0	—	—
700mμ Red	90.2	90.0	90.0	90.0	89.5	2.0	—
Total transmission	85.0	77.5	73.0	67.0	15.0	26.0	3.20

22. Storm Front, Jackson Hole, Wyoming. Here we have an impressive scene of rather low brightness range, and one which demanded some expansion of original contrast for interpretation of the desired mood. A K2 filter was used (there would be no appreciable advantage in using a stronger filter), and the distant mountains are rendered with adequate clarity. If the sky (upper right section) were darkened more than it is, it would have matched the ponderous deep-toned cloud mass on the left. The basic key value was the dark shore—it was visualized as Zone I—and the brightest areas of the cloud were expanded to between Zones VII and VIII. Less brilliancy would have created the impression of weakness; more contrast would have merely reduced the mood.

23. Silverton, Colorado. Orthochromatic rendering of a typical mountain scene. The pines are relatively lighter than with panchromatic film, and the sky is of fairly high value.

LANDSCAPE

Almost without exception, the farther an object lies from the camera, the more difficult it is to control and organize. Landscape is the supreme test of the photographer—and often the supreme disappointment. First, we have need of fortunate combinations of earth, sky, and cloud; we cannot "position" them, nor does our point of view admit of much flexibility (with a near subject, moving the camera only a few inches may make a profound change in its aspect). Second, we have the problem of haze, low color saturation, and scale. The last—scale—is perhaps the most important element of all. It is not only relative scale, but the impression of intrinsic scale, that is important. There are no rules to command this problem. It is a matter in sensitivity and perception; we must create the "presence" of the scene before us. In landscape work, we must strip the image of inessentials; the dismal "framing" of scenic views with tufts of fuzzy black branches should always be avoided. But the unity of near and far objects—compositionally speaking—is of extreme importance. Figures 5 and 27 in this book and Figure 30 in Book 1 suggest this near-far relationship.

The choice of lenses—focal lengths in relation to picture area—gives us considerable flexibility in adjusting physical scale to the area of our picture. A telephoto lens might reveal a great mountain or building in startling isolation; a wide-angle lens might show us a tremendous expanse of sky hovering over a distant range of snow peaks. Here is where visualization is of the utmost importance; many failures occur because of our *uncertainty* about the final image.

The impression of depth in space may sometimes be gained by or heightened by an intentional change of tonal values, through appropriate use of filters. In mountain photography, in which most elements of the subject are at a distance, the *optical* control of depth and perspective is limited. In lowland areas (especially in industrial environments), there is almost always a considerable amount of haze, which effectively separates various subject planes, even at moderate distances. The air in mountain or desert areas frequently has such great clarity that the atmospheric effect is minimized. Use of ordinary contrast filters here practically eliminates the illusion of depth. Other types of filters, however, can produce the desired effect by altering normal tonal relationships and creating exaggerated effects of distance and depth.

Before the advent of orthochromatic and panchromatic films photographic materials were sensitive to blue light only. Consequently the spectator was conditioned to accept white skies, dark foliage, and considerable atmospheric-haze effects as literal symbols of natural values. Magnificent images were nevertheless possible. It is difficult to imagine photographs of greater emotional impact than the early work of O'Sullivan in the American Southwest, or other outstanding landscape work of the period, in which the illusion of light and atmospheric space is imparted to an extraordinary extent. In his desire for photometric accuracy in color rendition, the modern photographer, even though he has such greatly improved materials, has sometimes lost a feeling for light and atmospheric depth. The symbolisms of today are no more "realistic" than those of the 1870s.

24a. El Capitan, Yosemite Valley. Made without filter.

We frequently see very dark skies, distances rendered with "airless" clarity, moving water frozen in time. All such effects are not literal records of experience, but actual stylized renderings inherently possible with the medium of photography.

In this panchromatic age we have forgotten the beauty of light skies and misty spaces. The clear blue sky is, photometrically speaking, equivalent to grays of about Zones V and VI values. At times we may wish to exaggerate its depth of tone; we use filters ranging from K1 to A—and on into the infrared; each stronger filter taking more light out of the sky but probably applying it to the objects *against* the sky—or *in* it. We seldom think of going the other way, of putting light into the sky to augment the mood of luminosity. This we can do with the blue filter. It is advised, for maximum feeling of light, that the general subject of the picture also be "high key" in character. Some experimentation will be well worth while. The Wratten C5 should be used.

Increasing the impression of atmospheric depth is another valuable function of the blue filter. I was once asked to photograph a vast forested basin and to reveal the various pine-covered ridges one beyond the other. To the eye it was practically impossible to distinguish these ridges; with panchromatic film and no filter only a slight aerial separation could be observed. But the blue filter produced a miraculous result; every massive forested ridge stood out clearly against the more distant one in progressively lighter values to the horizon. With the blue filter I had merely photographed the intervening air! This effect is suggested to a certain extent in Figure 24 a and b, only in this case I have tried to match the sky tone in both images by printing controls.

24b. El Capitan, Yosemite Valley. Made with C5 (blue) filter.

In telephotography, with the objects photographed at considerable distances from the camera, atmospheric effects are pronounced. The atmospheric effects themselves do not differ, regardless of the focal length of the lens used, and their logical accentuation as distance increases is often an advantage with images of ordinary angle of view. But in the telephoto image, the atmospheric effect may obscure desired detail, and the use of a relatively strong correction or contrast filter is indicated. The polarizer will frequently be of great help in eliminating haze effects.

As the focal length of the lens increases, high optical quality of the filter is of increasing importance. Image quality may be seriously degraded by inferior filters. When considerable magnification is used, filters must be either of the finest optical glass ("A" glass) or, better still, of plain gelatin foils which are so thin that they have no appreciable refraction, and thus serve the same purpose as the most finely ground filters at less cost and bulk. Furthermore, gelatin filters can be set between the lens components, which keeps them flat and dust-free.

Under ordinary atmospheric conditions use of such filters as the Wratten G, 23A, or 25A is advised. When separation of strong color values of distant objects is required, the Wratten No. 12 or G may be satisfactory, but when high contrast and much atmospheric clarification is desired, stronger filters should be used. A distant sunlit granite mountain peak, for example, rises against a sky that is close to the horizon and therefore far brighter than the sky appears toward the zenith. In other words, the blue of the sky close to the horizon is of a very low color saturation, and a very sharp-cut filter, such as a high-contrast red filter (Wratten F) must be used to separate the normal stone value from the sky value, if such separation is possible at all. The polarizer may be of great help in clarifying distant sky values. Striking effects are obtained by photographing *against* the light with relatively strong filters; the shadow values are clarified and made quite brilliant, while the sky behind the object appears very light, owing to its high brightness and low blue saturation.

25. Longs Peak, Colorado, on a Rainy Day. Made with blue filter (C5) to separate near ridge from the peak.

26. The Grand Teton (by Philip Knight), Telephotograph. This is a telephotograph of moderate magnification (equivalent focus 24 inches on a 4x5 negative) made with a Dallmeyer Adon lens. An A filter (gelatin) was used on Kodak Panatomic X film. Haze is almost eliminated; were some atmospheric effects desired, a No. 12 filter would have been selected. An F (No. 29) Wratten filter would have further increased the over-all contrast, but the sky values would have been lowered and undoubtedly "merged" with the shadow values of the cliffs. (Refer to Figure 30, where some merging is suggested). Note that the shadows on the foreground conifers are black, but that there is considerable glitter from the needles in sunlight. The red filter, absorbing green light, does transmit yellow light and of course the specular white reflections of the sun from the glossy pine needles.

47

27. Big Sur Coast, California. The composition revolves around the central black rock, which was visualized as of Zone I value. In the original print there is a great variety of tonalities in sand, water, and sky. Sunset colors prevented my achieving a deeper sky tone.

48

SEASCAPE

Subjects classified under the generalized term of "seascape" are, of course, of unlimited number. The same principles apply as with ordinary landscape, except for certain qualities peculiar to ocean and shore. Esthetic considerations aside, the ocean and its colors are perceived chiefly in terms of reflection from the sky. If the sky is an intense, clear blue, the color of the water is of a modified blue, depending, of course, upon its purity or its turbulence. If the sky is overcast, the color of the ocean becomes a deep gray-green, or even, at times, almost colorless. Qualities of the ocean floor in relatively shallow regions affect surface color; also, the angle of view always has much to do with the apparent color of the water.

Optically, any extensive view of the ocean demands extreme precision of detail; its textures, though close in value, must be retained in the final image. This is especially true in the sheen of sunlight on wave crests, which both factually and emotionally is very sharp and incisive. Tide rips and bands of subtly different colors can be accentuated by increasing the contrast in the image through reduced exposure and increased development, and/or by the use of appropriate filters.

The blue of the ocean responds almost the same as the blue of the sky to yellow, orange, and red filters. Now we have learned to accept skies of very deep tone in black-and-white photography, but it is difficult to tolerate overexaggerated depth of tone of the ocean in general seascapes. In fact, it is seldom that a filter more powerful than a K2 is required, except under conditions of haze or when dramatic cloudscapes are prominent. The atmospheric effect is ordinarily a continuous lightening of tone toward the horizon; there is no such sharp demarcation between values as one finds in mountains, where range after range may stand out in definite relief, one against the other. If this atmospheric effect is completely eliminated by too strong filters, the ocean loses perspective and the effect of recession, appearing almost as a wall—a single tone beneath the sky. Furthermore, as the water's turbulence increases, the various reflective angles of the waves, especially in rather acute angles to the sun, allow very interesting textural treatment, but the use of an overstrong filter in such circumstances produces strange granular effects.

All the foregoing refers to a point of view of considerable height, from the deck of a ship or a high bluff, below which a vast expanse of ocean can be seen. In photographs of the sea taken from the shore the most difficult problem lies in arresting the flow of water and the motion of near waves to the proper degree. As in the photography of all moving forms in nature, the basic structure of the scene must be decisively sharp, and against this precision some wave motion may be discreetly indicated. An extremely high-speed photograph of a cresting wave would certainly not convey the impression of substance or energy, yet the other extreme of a complete blur that destroys the illusion of substance must be avoided also. In capturing bursting spray from rocks, the ideal moment of exposure is just before the spray burst reaches its crest. Considerable experience is necessary to anticipate the most impressive moments for breakers, since the photographer must be hair-trigger alert for the moment when the moving forms combine significantly. It is exceedingly difficult under any conditions to photograph foam and preserve its minute detail and texture. A long-focus lens is helpful in photographing most sea phenomena, with shutter speeds of 1/500 second and higher.

The polarizer is often an invaluable aid in penetrating the surface of quiet pools to reveal details within. See page 32 for comment on the polarizer; also refer to Book 1 on the care of camera and lenses, as salt spray and sea air are harmful to cameras and accessories.

The photography of shore sand, sand dunes, weathered rock and wood, shells, seaweed, and the flotsam and jetsam of the sea may be classed as minutiae of nature. The precise rendition of texture is important; there is nothing more distressing than out-of-focus images of sand. In fact, the definition of sand and foam images presents a serious problem; in contact prints such minute details can be retained, but in enlargements they may conflict with image grain (see Book 1, page 34).

The exposure problems for all general subjects connected with the sea are not difficult, at least as far as shadow values are concerned. There is a good, broad illumination, with shadows strongly reinforced by a great open source of light from sky and sea. The skies along the seacoast are usually more opaque than at high altitudes. The color of the reflected skylight contains less blue light and consequently may be less susceptible to the usual effect of correcting filters.

Shadow values should have sufficiently high placement on the exposure scale to avoid harshness. An efficient lens hood is necessary because of the large amount of enveloping reflected light. When there are exceptionally bright reflections in the water, unwanted flare and ghost images may result from photographing directly into the sun. As the source of these defects lies chiefly within the field of view, the lens hood has no power to correct them. A coated lens is of great help in reducing these otherwise unavoidable effects. Internal reflective surfaces of the camera can cause severe flare. Needless to say, in taking meter readings of water surfaces you must be extremely careful to avoid including any definite reflection of the sun itself in the field of the meter, since the readings will then be quite inaccurate. Suggestions for an approximate placement of values on the exposure scale are as follows:

Reasonably blue sky near the horizon, Zone VI; blue sky near the north zenith, Zone V; surface of the ocean, Zones IV-V; quality of average beach sand, Zones V-VI; shadow under waves, Zones II-III; foam, Zones VII-VIII; reflections of sunlight on water, Zone IX or higher. Orthochromatic film is entirely adequate for average seascapes, but as it records the blue of the sea in a lighter tone than panchromatic film, a K1 or K2 filter can be consistently used, or reduced exposure with related increased development employed, to expand and separate otherwise close values.

Exposure problems under conditions of storm and fog are not much different from those of general landscape under similar conditions. A somewhat massive negative is indicated, for gray masses of fog and clouds must be rendered with smoothness of tone.

Most photographs of the sea should have a quality of lightness and crispness, suggesting transparent illumination. Heavy blue-green, olive-green, and brownish print tones should be avoided, and the use of obvious blue and green colors can be seriously questioned from an esthetic viewpoint. To my mind, the mood of the sea is best expressed by a sharp, neutral black fortified with a touch of cold purple sepia. It is not required that the actual colors of the scene be interpreted, but that a feeling of clarity and brilliance be conveyed.

28. Upper Yosemite Fall, Yosemite Valley. An example of various tempos of falling water; some parts of the fall are very sharp, others slightly blurred. A K2 filter was used, fairly low placement of brightnesses, and expanded development. Actually the brightest part of the scene is the glistening wet rock to the right of the top of the fall. The fall itself, being of broken masses of water, was less bright than the smooth continuous sheen of the wet rock. This photograph was made with the camera pointed severely upward; however, it was *horizontally* level, and the orientation is correct.

STILL AND MOVING WATER

Water, while quite transparent, has considerable reflective powers, as everyone who has stood by a still pool must know. Rocks, trees, buildings, and sky are reflected with startling clarity and brilliance in a still, deep pool. The bed of a shallow clear pool may appear very definite to both eye and lens; the pool bed and the environmental reflections combine in intricate and often confusing patterns. The polarizer will reduce the surface reflections to a marked degree, but if these surface reflections are entirely removed, the impression of the *substance* of water will be seriously affected. As the surface of the water becomes rippled and broken by wind or for other reasons, the effect of transparency is reduced and the surface reflections become chaotic. A short exposure will preserve the broken chaotic details, and the image will approximate what the eye sees. A longer exposure will blend these broken reflections into a more or less smooth and indefinite impression of reflections—blurred and quite obviously unreal—especially so if the objects reflected also appear in the field of view.

As the degree of motion of the water surface increases, the reflections become more chaotic, and finally you are aware more of a rapidly changing textured surface than of "reflections." At this point a myriad random highlights—scintillations from the sun—may appear. These scintillations are rather rapid in sequence and of very short duration. A very quick exposure will show these scintillations as they appear within a short interval of time, and the movement of the water will be frozen. A longer exposure will serve to superimpose several patterns of scintillations, and you will achieve some impressions of flow and movement of the water. Too long exposure will superimpose too many scintillations, and a general impression of blocking and blurring will obtain.

In my opinion, an exposure showing the actual flow of a stream or the dashing water in cascades should be short enough to render every essential detail of the image with considerable sharpness, but not so short that the motion of the water is completely arrested. Moving water "frozen" by very high shutter speeds assumes the appearance of glass and is completely static. Analyze a rushing cascade, examine various parts closely. You see an underlying forward rush of water of rather smooth and consistent reflective value. This is fringed with foam, but the greatest disturbance derives from underlying rocks and obstructions. Here the water is frequently stopped, and rolls back or is thrown back over the basic flow of the current. In these areas you get definite upthrows of water in a boiling effect, with drops thrown into the air. If you give a short exposure, completely stopping all motion, the result is quite unnatural. It is best to expose so as to render the boiling and tossing drops quite sharply, at the same time allowing a slight blur to persist in the swift underlying flow.

The brightness values of white water vary considerably according to the direction of light. The average white cascade in flat hazy skylight is from 200 to 400 c.p.sq.ft. In sunlight it approaches 1,600 c.p.sq.ft. and more. In either case, white water should be visualized as very light in the print, but never so light that the textural values are completely lost. The placement is actually on Zone VIII for the mass of white water. Any specular reflections of the sun must, of course, be considerably higher (Zone IX in the print or higher in the negative). It must be emphasized that the deeper tonalities of the water should not be rendered too dark; there must always be a feeling of transparency and translucency along with that of substance. Otherwise the realistic impression of water will be lost. White water photographed in shade is very difficult to render in any way except as either a blank white or a pasty gray. If this must be attempted, it is best to keep the values high on the scale. It is also rather difficult, when working in flat sunlight, to "separate" white water from light sand or stone. I advise lower zonal placement and increased development. Against the sun there is a vastly greater range of tonalities. Waterfalls should be photographed in oblique light as much as possible, in order to point up form and texture.

Water moving across the field of view obviously must be given shorter exposure than water flowing to or from the camera. However, water flowing away from the camera usually is less effective photographically. I advise photographing cascades at an oblique angle. Exposures depend upon distance of object, size of image, and so on. With the ordinary camera at a distance of 20 feet, 1/200 second usually suffices. A waterfall at a distance of a mile is adequately stopped at $\frac{1}{10}$ second; at a distance of a few hundred feet a very high shutter speed may be required. In photographing waterfalls, as in cascades, compromise between stopping the motion and obtaining a continuous blur. Remember that the motion of the mass of water is very much greater than the motion of mist and spray. Whereas the motion of a waterfall is continuous, gathering speed from the moment of its initial leap, that of a geyser may be discontinuous, and near the crest of the spurt is of quite low velocity. Geyser steam is vague in shape and texture; as with the driving mists of waterfalls, it should be rendered with delicacy.

It is sometimes possible to achieve interesting effects by multiple exposures of moving water. Usually, the exposures should be very short, as the superimposed images should be sharp—although it might be possible to give a fairly long exposure (to show movement and blur) and then add one or more very short exposures giving "frozen" images. The ratio of exposure times in multiple-exposure photographs varies with the subject. As a rule, the final negative should show normal all-over opacity. If most of the subject is light, compute the normal exposure value for a single exposure and distribute this value over the multiple exposures. If the subject is of mixed tonalities, such as a foaming cascade, showing dark pools and rocks, etc., and if the position of the bright spurts of foam will vary against the darker background, I suggest you give a "normal" exposure for each of the superimposed images.

Foam patterns on dark water also provide exciting opportunities for single and multiple-exposure compositions.

Falling water appears blue in its shadowed parts. This blue can be deepened by the use of yellow filters, but it is important that it never be deepened too much. In revealing the maximum texture of waterfalls it is better to lower zonal placement and increase development rather than to rely on contrast filters, which tend to produce a "flour-and-soot" image. When using filters in photographing quiet streams, lakes, and pools, remember that a yellow filter may darken the water, which as a rule is reflecting the blue of the sky. If it is necessary to *raise* the value of these water surfaces, a blue filter is indicated. In forest pools, which reflect green, the relative value of the water can be raised by using yellow-green or green filters. Water appears more transparent if a polarizer is used, but the polarizer may reduce or eliminate important reflections.

Rain pools usually reflect the sky with considerable brightness. If rain is falling on pool surfaces, the exposure should be fast enough to render the splash effect with clarity. Rain pools on dark stone, wood, or pavements are, together with their immediate environment, of rather low key—except for the direct reflections of sky, light clouds, and buildings, and the sun or other light sources. Care should be exercised not to place the dark environment values too low. Dark wet stone, for example, is of quite low brightness, but it is seldom *black* in actuality or mood.

Objects that are wet have lower diffuse reflectivity, but higher "specular" reflectivity. In measuring the brightnesses of wet surfaces, do not include direct reflections of the sun or other light sources in the field of the meter; otherwise the readings will be too high and underexposure will result.

Rain *can be* photographed with adequate exposure speeds; it is especially effective in stereo images. The impression of rain is not the revelation of separate drops (quite impossible except with high-speed lights), but the general mood of "wetness," diffuse streaks of rain, mist, and stormy distance. Rain and dewdrops on leaves, when photographed close at hand, show exciting optically distorted reflections of the environment.

Storm effects, especially common in the American Southwest, in which dark sheets of rain are seen falling against distant clear skies, can be strikingly photographed by use of a moderate filter (K2 or No. 12), and with reduced exposure and increased development.

Rainbows, easy to record on color film, are not easy to interpret in black-and-white photography. It is important that the rainbow be seen in strong contrast with a dark background, such as a brooding thunderstorm sky. Conditions under which rainbows appear are definite; the sun must be shining on falling rain or mist. The radius of the rainbow is about $41°$ of arc; that is, it subtends $41°$ from the axis of the sun. Its position can be anticipated by noting where the shadow of your head falls, and then describing in space an arc of $41°$ radius around it. Distance does not change this angle; distant rain or the spray from a near-by cascade will produce rainbows on the same arc from the sun's axis. A secondary rainbow (weaker than the principal one) may be observed at about $52°$ from the sun's axis.

The intensity of the rainbow depends upon the concentration of the falling rain and the intensity of the sun. (It is also effectively exaggerated by the tonal depth of the background.) As it contains all the colors of the spectrum, the intensity of its image depends upon the sensitivity of the film and the filters used. (Panchromatic film is strongly indicated.) I have found that a K2 filter is sufficient if the exposure is short, and the development more than normal. If stronger filters are used, the width of the rainbow is lessened—the blue band is weakened by yellow filters, both blue and red bands by green filters, and the red-orange band by blue filters. A red filter would obviously transmit only the red band, and while the image might be quite brilliant, its width would be unnaturally thin. I have never been able to make a satisfactory image of a rainbow without using a filter. The polarizer will have no effect on the background of a rainbow, because the angle to the sun is wrong. For exposure, I suggest that the background be placed on Zone III—not higher than Zone IV—and normal-plus development be given the negative.

SNOW AND ICE

Ideally, it should not be necessary to discuss various subjects when expounding photographic theory and technique, because with a full command of technique any subject is manageable within the limitations of the medium itself. In a purely physical sense a subject is simply a variety of brightnesses, and planned exposure and development of the negative merely establish these brightnesses in terms of opacities appropriate to the desired values of the final print. However, I am not concerned with mere physical relationships; the imaginative and emotional factors dominate. Hence my technique is largely applied to problems of *interpretation* rather than to factual transcription—interpretation based upon visualization.

Winter photography is difficult not because of any particular problems of brightness, contrast, etc., but rather because the emotional interpretation of snow is highly subjective and relates to values of the utmost subtlety. In sunlit snow scenes you are confronted with an impression of enveloping light; actually contrasts may be severe, but the general impression is one of crisp, luminous brilliancy. All too often you see harsh, chalky photographs of snow subjects—blocked high values and inky shadows. Or you see the "pictorial" extreme—soft fuzzy gray images without clarity or vitality.

Snow in shade is particularly difficult to manage; the values are extremely close, and the results are either too dull and flat or too blank and washed-out.

Granted that you should preserve the conviction of substance and light in snow scenes and their details under all lighting conditions, just how do you begin to think about the problem?

First, consider substance. Snow is brilliant, crystalline, and usually presents softly modulated contours. It may define planes and edges of the forms on which it falls, but in general it is smooth and gently rounded, never abrupt, as may be the case with ice.

Second, consider its brightness scale—the impression of luminosity. Snow in bright sunlight will measure 1600 c.p.sq.ft. and more; the reflective glare of sun on snow may be much higher—3000 c.p.sq.ft. and more. Shadowed snow, depending upon exposure to open sky, is at most one-fourth as bright; in open forest it will be about one-eighth the brightness of sunlit snow. But the "feeling" of shadowed snow is one of enveloping light, and the relationship of shadowed to sunlit snow in the print usually must be closer than in actuality if the mood is to be preserved.

Snow in flat light retains the feeling of whiteness, and it is important that the image should not appear flat or muddied in tone.

Trees, rocks, buildings, are usually very much darker than snow, but the reflections from the snow, plus the general mood of enveloping light, make it important not to render them too dark. A wooden building in shade should not fall below Zone III in the print; in fact, the deepest significant shadow should not be placed below Zone III on the exposure scale if any impression of substance is to be preserved. If an object in shade measures 25 c.p.sq.ft., and is placed on Zone III, snow in sun (1600 c.p.sq.ft.) falls on Zone IX and normal-minus development is indicated, as sunlit snow should average Zone VIII or a little below to reveal textures and tonal variations. Small shadowed areas, such as tree

29. Yosemite Forest, Winter. At first glance one might think this subject was one of very high contrast (great brightness range). Due to the fact that there was much environmental reflection from surrounding snow-covered ground and trees and that the trees also received uninterrupted light from the open north sky, the actual brightness range was not excessive. The tree on the right registered at least 50 c.p.sq.ft., the one on the left about 13 c.p.sq.ft., and the darker tree in the background about 6.5 c.p.sq.ft. The snow in shade about 200 c.p.sq.ft. and the snow in sun about 1600. The problem was to keep the lower values separated so as to preserve the impression of luminosity; the snow in sun could go very light. The 6.5 value was placed on Zone II, and the negative was developed in the two-solution formula (page 78).

trunks and rocks at some distance, can be rendered as Zone II or even Zone I, but any important significant shadow area must be adequately revealed.

Open snow landscapes, while very bright, will have a rather small brightness range: for example, sunlit snow fields, 1600 plus; blue sky, 200; clouds, 800 plus; snow in shade, 200-400; maximum range 1:8. (This, please note, does not include trees, buildings, rocks, etc.) A K2 filter reduces the values of the sky and shaded snow about 2x; this makes the brightness range 1:16. If the snow in sun is rendered on Zone VIII, the sky will be on Zone IV, and the scene will have good luminosity. If a G filter is used, the sky and shaded snow are reduced in value about two zones (4x), and the brightness range is about 1:32. The sky falls on Zone III, and the mood may be too deep and cold. Stronger filters would merely give such exaggerations of values that all impression of substance and light would be lost. In my opinion the Wratten No. 12 filter is about the strongest that can be used without unduly exaggerating naturalistic values.

As not only the broad shadows on snow, but the minute shadows within the snow, are bluish, a yellow or a red filter will intensify the textural qualities to a marked degree. A K2 or a No. 12 will not be too strong if normal placements are given the values. If the texture is overexaggerated, the snow loses its delicate quality; it becomes very granular and coarse. Also, modulations in the surface of a large snow area become more abrupt, and the impression of light is lost.

To *condense* the scale, I advise a C5 (blue) filter; this not only raises the values of the shaded snow but slightly reduces the values of the sunlit snow. Normal-plus development is usually indicated when a C5 filter is used (see p. 21).

A polarizer will reduce reflections at the optimum angle to the snow, but the effect is not always a happy one. The scintillations from the snow crystals lend much to the general conviction of substance, and when these are removed a flourlike quality is obtained.

With snow in shade a K2 or a No. 12 filter will intensify the differences of brightness—both gross and minute—but the effect may be quite unpleasant; granular textures and depressed areas of tone are the inevitable effect of over-filtering and insufficient exposure. The deeper you see into a mass of snow or one of ice, the bluer becomes its substance, and a strong filter will severely exaggerate this effect. In other words, keep all values in a snow scene buoyant and full of light.

I cannot stress too much the importance of proper placement of high values. If bright objects are visualized as bright, they demand a high placement. An average meter reading of a snow scene might be 1,000 c.p.sq.ft. although the brightness of the sunlight snow was 1600 c.p.sq.ft., of shadowed snow, 200 c.p.sq.ft., and of a building in shade, 25 c.p.sq.ft. If you simply place the average reading of 1000 opposite the arrow of the Weston Master Meter (Zone V of the exposure scale), you will grossly underexpose the scene; the building falls below Zone O, the shadowed snow below Zone III, and the sunlit snow between Zones V and VI. If you place the average reading on the C of the meter—Zone VI—you still have underexposure to contend with; the building falls between Zones O and I, and the shaded snow under Zone IV. The sunlit snow falls between Zones VI and VII. But the shaded snow can be placed one zone higher (on about Zone V) and that would bring the building closer to Zone II. The sunlit snow would then fall on or near Zone VIII, and about normal development would be indicated.

30. Pine Tree and Snow, Yosemite. Edgings of sunlit snow prevent some tonal mergers with the values of the blue sky.

Ice presents about the same general problems as snow, except that you have much more definite forms and sharp highlights. The highlights are always much brighter than the diffuse reflections, which are lower than those of snow masses. The measured brightness (average) of icicles in sun may be placed on Zone VI, that of icicles in shade on Zone V. In both cases normal-plus development is suggested. Glare on ice fields is strong, and it may be advisable to control it somewhat with the polarizer.

Portraits and figures on snow will have considerable illumination in the shadows reflected from below, and there should be little trouble holding values in the shadowed parts of the face (the range should be about 1:4). In ski-action photographs, care should be taken to give sufficient exposure to give *at least* Zone IV value to the shadowed parts of the face—Zone V would be better. To avoid confusion, remember that snow in open shade is illuminated by direct light from the sky and the proportion of sunlit and shaded brightness is the same as for any other substance. But objects above or near to snow have both the light from the open sky *and* the reflections from the snow, and the shadows may be illuminated to a startling degree.

Snow and foliage are favored by the use of a green filter, such as the XI. Late sunset colors on snow will be rendered too light with yellow and orange filters unless a less-than-normal exposure factor is used.

31. Snow Hummocks, Yosemite. Textures enhanced by filtering, reduced exposure, and expanded development.

FOLIAGE

Nothing so definitely reveals the difference between visual and photographic values as does the photography of foliage with panchromatic film. The eye perceives yellow-green more acutely than other colors of the spectrum. Hence the use of yellowish-green safelights in the darkroom in preference to red ones; the volume of light useful to the eye in the yellow-green range would be almost invisible in the red range. Unfortunately, the photographic film does not have this high sensitivity to green. Orthochromatic film shows the highest response, but this is still considerably lower than its response to blue light. Panchromatic film, especially the Type C film, has a rather low sensitivity to green light. These facts account for the rather dark rendering of foliage in relation to other colors of apparently equal visual brightness.

Foliage is comprised of a great variety of colors. Dark conifers tend more to the bluish-green; bright poplars and maples have a definitely yellow-green hue. As we have seen in the section on filters, use of a red filter on foliage has not the same effect as its use on an object of a pure monochromatic green. This is because the foliage is not of high color saturation, and reflects a large percentage of white light.

Visually, the separation of foliage from other objects in the landscape depends largely upon color contrasts. In a landscape viewed through a monochromatic filter, the average foliage lies on or below the middle tones of the scale. This natural low placement is exaggerated by the film's inadequate sensitivity to green and the photographer's tendency to underexpose through averaging the light values. It is easy to understand, then, why the results are so often darker than the photographer intended. This inherent low brightness of foliage plus the intricate internal shadows present a very definite problem. Refer to Figure 2.

Another factor that complicates the image of foliage lies in the composite effect of specular highlights, reflected diffuse light, and minute shadows. Most people think of a tree as just a green object and never pause to analyze the derivation of its color and tones. We know that a texture remains apparent as such only within the limits of visual resolution. Thus if you look at a tree from far off you see it as an object of rather broad masses of green light and shade. But as you come nearer to the tree, the individual leaves or needles are revealed. and you become aware of its textural complexity. You note further that a good part of it is in rather deep shadow, for not only are there the broad shadows opposite the light source, but also the thousands of minute shadows cast by the leaves, one upon the other. In addition, each leaf reflects a highlight, the brightness of which depends on whether it is derived from sunlight or from diffuse daylight. When you take a meter reading of the tree, you are therefore measuring the average of a complex grouping of highlights, diffuse light, and shadow, and as a rule this average reading is only about 50% of the brightness of the fully illuminated leaves in flat lighting. The larger proportion of shadows has cut down the average, and as the angle of light becomes more acute, the areas in shadow are augmented. Lens and camera flare will modify the tonalities of minute shadow areas, raising their values relatively to the brightness of the area photographed and of the surrounding environment. Photometric measurements (from the camera position) will indicate the actual brightnesses of small areas of light and shadow.

I advise that you practice judging the approximate proportion of shadowed to sunlit areas in all your subject matter, especially in subjects of intricate form and texture. In visualizing the image of a tree you must not overlook the important tonalities of the shadows. An "average" meter reading will not determine the values of the shadows or of the fully illuminated areas; it will give only the averaged reflectivity of the subject. A spot meter—such as the S.E.I., with a very narrow angle of view—will indicate the values of small shadows and sunlit areas. Creating an artificial shadow (with a hat or a large cardboard) will suggest the values of the shadows at, or close to, the *surface* of the foliage; it will not give the values of the shadows deep within the body of the tree. However, the deeper shadows—usually very small in the image—can be rendered as complete black if the important near-surface shadows possess some firm tone in the image. If all the shadows within a tree are completely black, the effect is harsh and destroys the illusion of light that is so desirable in the vast majority of interpretations. Also, the high relative sensitivity of the eye to green intensifies an impression of brightness of the shadowed green foliage that is very difficult to convey in the photograph.

When filters are used with foliage, caution must be exercised not to produce a harsh "chalk-and-charcoal" effect. Yellow and green filters will raise the values of the sunlit areas, but lower the values of the shadows, since the latter are largely illuminated by scattered blue light and very low value green light. Orange and red filters will slightly lower the values of green leaves, and of course will exaggerate the depth of shadow values. Specular highlights on leaves will always be rendered in high value with or without filters, as they are composed of light of the full spectrum. (However, a polarizer will reduce these sharp reflections to any predetermined visual degree.) When the foliage is in soft diffuse light, or in full shade, filters will have less contrast effect than in sunlight, but the values of the green foliage will be raised when yellow, green, or yellow-green filters are employed. A filter transmits its own color to the maximum degree; the higher the color saturation of a green leaf, the more effective a green or a yellow-green filter will be. But, as was mentioned before, most foliage has rather low color saturation, and the response to filters is not very pronounced.

Therefore, to create in the photograph an impression of the visual appearance of foliage, you must take these elements into consideration:

1. The high (relatively) sensitivity of the eye to green light
2. The low-to-moderate color saturation of green foliage
3. The relatively low sensitivity of panchromatic film to green light. This would indicate that if you visualize a foliage value as a Zone V value in the print you should place the metered value of the foliage on Zone VI—one zone higher. (If orthochromatic film is used, place one-half zone higher.)

When other conditions permit, a more "luminous" rendition of foliage will be obtained when the metered values are placed two zones higher on the scale and reduced development-time is given the negative; this will favor the shadow values and preserve the "illusion of light." In working with foliage against blue sky it is often difficult to preserve the emotional contrast of green against blue in terms of black-and-white values. A definite contrast of tone—rendering the tree either considerably darker or considerably lighter than the sky—is necessary. Two or three zones of effective separation are required. A blue filter will darken the foliage and lighten the sky. Perhaps the best solution of this problem is to use a monochromatic green filter (such as the Wratten B). Place the sunlit values of the foliage on Zone V, multiply the exposure by the published factor of the green filter, and develop the negative to a "normal-plus" degree. The result will approximate the following differences of value: blue sky, Zone IV; sunlit foliage, Zones VI-VII. For dark coniferous foliage (somewhat bluish-green of low saturation) the sunlit foliage, placed on Zone V as above, may not exceed Zone V½ in the print; in such cases, give longer development time to achieve greater contrast.

In photographing foliage close at hand the highlights on the leaves may appear quite brilliant and should be rendered as pure white in the print, except when the area of the highlight is large and some suggestion of substance is required; then the highlight area should show modulation of value—only the most intense reflective area should be rendered as pure white. In cases of extreme contrast, alternate water-bath or compensating development should be given the negative (see Book 2) so as to preserve some illusion of substance and luminosity. Everyone is familiar with the "lunar" quality of foliage that has been rendered overharsh.

Autumn foliage is intrinsically more brilliant than average green foliage, and as a rule the yellows and reds are of much higher color saturation. The use of K2, No. 12, and G filters will greatly augment the effect of brilliance of the leaves, but the proportionate deepening of the shadows at the same time is likely to create overharsh contrasts. Red filters will create much greater contrast, and unrealistic effects, and should be used with caution. I have found that the most satisfactory effects with autumn foliage are achieved by using a No. 12 or a G filter with a higher factor than normal and giving the negative reduced development. Say that you desire the average values of the autumn leaves to appear in the print as Zone VII value: Place the brightness value of the leaves on Zone VI and use a G filter with a factor of 4 instead of 2½ or 3. This will render the yellow-orange leaves about 1½ zones higher. (Remember, a filter passes light of its own color with but slight absorption.) Reducing the development time will serve to render the leaf values on about Zone VII. Now the shadows will also have been raised a bit above normal and the final result is one of less all-over contrast, but high luminosity. In such subjects as a spray of autumn leaves against the blue sky, when there is a minimum of shadow on the leaves themselves, exactly the opposite procedure can be followed; a K2 or No. 12 or G filter can be used without any exposure factor, and the development time increased. This effectively lowers the sky value two or three zones, and the leaf values only about one-half zone. If the effective placement of the brightness value of autumn leaves is not above Zone VI, prolonged development will not block the image.*

Flowers

Flowers are usually of higher color saturation than average green foliage. It is difficult to read the actual value of small flowers except with a "spot" photometer, but a gray card will be helpful when it is practicable to establish a middle-gray value. This middle-gray value is useful in color photography, but with black-and-white photography much experience is required to visualize just how

---

* By "effective" brightness I mean the calculated brightness of the subject, with due consideration for the filter effect.

the flower colors are to be rendered in the print. Close images of flowers on growing plants present exacting problems: backgrounds, excessively contrasty shadows, wind motion, optical limitations, and distortions of scale. I suggest the use of lenses with very long focus whenever possible, windbreaks, and reflectors. The latter two can be combined, and the windbreak be made of light cardboard or cheesecloth screens. Sometimes artificial backgrounds of neutral-colored cards are absolutely necessary, although flowers against bark, rock, or large leaves may create interesting (if botanically questionable) compositions.

Trees, grasses, and flowers are fine textural and formal objects in the photographic sense, and it is essential that they be always presented with a clear precision. The motion produced by wind will often ruin definition and textural quality. You must watch carefully to observe small wind movements over the entire area of the picture. I have frequently set the shutter on B (Bulb) and exposed intermittently—awaiting moments when no wind movement was to be perceived. However, if the wind is of adequate force to displace leaves and flowers permanently the intermittent exposure method will not work.

There is nothing as satisfactory in dealing with these objects as working in a large greenhouse or conservatory; the soft lighting and the still air permit long exposures of flowers and leaves. The quality of the light (through the whitened glass) may have considerable effect with color films, but will have little practical effect with black-and-white materials.

In working with mosses, lichens, and other objects of very low color saturation, it will usually be necessary to create exaggerated contrast by side lighting or low zonal placement and prolonged development. Do not forget to calculate for excessive lens extension when working with close subjects, and do not overlook the reciprocity effect with long exposures (see Book 2).

Roots, Dead Trees, and Bark

The shapes of natural objects such as trees and shrubs are often obscured by the living leaves and bark. In death, trees and branch forms are spectacular in their simplicity of shape and richness of texture. It is not a sentimental choice between a magnificent living tree and a dead one; it is just that such subjects lend themselves to the photographic interpretation and become, in a sensitive print, objects of exceptional interest and beauty. (Refer to Fig. 18 herein, and to Fig. 11, Book 2). As the colors of such objects are usually faint—chiefly light gray to white—separation of wood and sky values must be carefully visualized and checked. A dead tree may appear as solid as a rock, but it can sway in the wind, and such motion is very hard to see against a blue sky. Roots (see Fig. 8) and fragments of wood possess extraordinary composition potentials. And the bark of many trees: eucalyptus, pine, madrone, etc., can be photographed excitingly. Burned wood (Fig. 18), which is chiefly charcoal, reflects a very low value of diffuse light, but has a bright glistening highlight; ordinary close meter readings may be falsely high owing to these highlights. The black charcoal should be placed on about Zones I or II. With close details, Zone III—even IV—would be appropriate.

Wood and stone, while of usually different colors, will frequently photograph in the same monochromatic value. Only by strong lighting effects and adequate image contrast can these values be differentiated (see Fig. 85, Book 3).

DESERT PHOTOGRAPHY

As the distances encountered in desert landscapes are usually very great, atmospheric effects can be pronounced, justifying the use of stronger filters than normal with average landscape. On the other hand, the air may often be very clear, but if so, the great distances will be quite bluish and demand the use of a blue-absorbing filter, such as a K2 or a No. 12, to obtain even a "normal" atmospheric effect. Dramatic interpretations may require the use of strong filters such as the G, but filters such as the A, F, and infrared should be used with caution. The dominant mood of the desert is one of light and brilliance, and strong filters tend to give "lunar" effects—harsh shadows and glaring high values. Blue skies rendered too dark also destroy the illusion of light.

Most of the American desert—with the exception of the more colorful areas of the Southwest—is of rather low color contrast, and the values of the desert mountains, softened by atmospheric effects, closely approximate the values of the sky (except when photographed against the light). It is quite a problem to determine just how much contrast control should be applied to create the impression of clarity and yet preserve the important mood of light. Perhaps the most practical solution is to use filters of moderate strength and obtain more contrast by fairly low placement of the subject brightnesses on the exposure scale, and related "normal-plus" development. In subjects with small shadow areas the values can be averaged and placed on Zone V, but near objects in sun and shadow may be very contrasty, and the shadow values must be respected. On the other hand, the vast open skies and the high reflectivity of some desert rock and sand may give considerable reflected illumination of the shadow areas. The glare of the desert environment may confuse the eye and give a false impression of the relative brightnesses of shadow and sunlit areas. Careful determination of brightnesses by a light meter is always advised.

The effect of light in terms of mood and brilliancy peculiar to the desert is often achieved by visualizing the subject in a fairly high key, but with small shadows visualized very black. The edges of telegraph poles, fence posts, bushes, and stones—even those of hill forms—can be renderd an intense black. Of course, if large areas appear as black, a "lunar" effect results. By a "large shadow" I refer to a shadowed area that demands internal detail to "read" well; a small shadow can be "understood" by form and position in the subject area.

The desert under snow is extraordinarily beautiful; usually the distances are of great clarity. The same general techniques applicable to snow photography (page 55) can be applied. Frequently the desert regions are afflicted with great dust storms; while they are in progress it is best to protect the camera and lenses securely and bide your time. Not even infrared techniques will make much impression on the all-enveloping dust. It is obvious that the most exciting play of light and shadow will take place very early and late in the day, but to the accomplished photographer there is no time of day in which he cannot photograph effectively. It requires an acute visualization to realize form and tonal separations under completely flat lighting, yet some of Edward Weston's most effective photographs are those of the desert (Death Valley) made at high noon without benefit of clouds. The variation of colors in Death Valley, the Grand Canyon, and similar regions permits striking compositions under most lighting conditions if strong filters are intelligently employed. The following suggestions may be of value:

1. Yellowish rock may be rendered very light against blue sky with a K2, a No. 12, or a G filter, especially if the filters are used without their standard exposure factors. Remember, filters freely transmit light of their own colors. When using a yellow filter on yellow rock without applying an exposure factor, we will find that the yellow rock will be recorded as almost the same opacity in the negative as when the filter is not used. But other values—especially the blues and colors with blue components—will be darkened to a greater extent than if an exposure factor were applied with normal exposure. Approximately, if a yellow filter reduced sky value from Zone VI to Zone V (with normal exposure and application of the filter factor), it might, with normal exposure and no multiplying factor, further lower the sky value to Zone IV. Also, we should clarify the statement that a filter freely transmits its own color (and modifies other colors). That is quite true with the monochromats, but with the yellow filters there is transmission of most of the visible spectrum excepting in the blue and the violet regions. Let us think of a vista of the Grand Canyon—red and yellow cliffs, dark-green trees, blue sky, and haze. With panchromatic film and various filters we can visualize the picture with considerable variation of color values. Refer to the transmission tables on page 41.

2. Reddish rock will be rendered darker with a green filter, as will blue sky.

3. The use of a blue filter will lighten the sky and render most rocks deeper in tone, but its most important effect is to create atmospheric perspective. On clear days recessive ridges and ranges may be impossible to separate except with a blue filter (which literally photographs the intervening air). (See Fig. 24.)

4. The polarizer is very effective in lowering the values of the sky and of the distant hazy landscape. It will also accentuate delicate clouds. But it may also modify the glare from crystalline mineral deposits, and this effect should be carefully observed before exposing.

5. Desert clouds are usually delicate in form and texture, but that does not imply that they should be brutally exaggerated by the use of strong contrast filters.

6. The greens of plants and trees in desert country are usually of very low color saturation. with the exception of deciduous trees in moist places, and will not be much affected by filters. Sage, rabbit brush, and most varieties of cactus approach a neutral-gray tonality with a minimum response to all filters. However, a green filter such as the Wratten No. 58 (Tricolor B) will serve to give good values to sky and rock, and will have some effect on the desert foliage. Greater depth of sky can be achieved by adding the polarizer to the green filter.

There is no doubt that the most exciting effects are obtained by photographing into the sun—or at least at an acute angle toward the sun. Proper shading of the lens from the direct rays of the sun is most important, and a fully coated lens is always indicated. With this lighting, relief and depth are more positively revealed, near forms—rocks, trees, plants—acquire interesting edge lighting, and if values are properly balanced, a beautiful mood of light and space will be achieved.

It is not out-of-place here to reiterate the need for protection of equipment and supplies in a desert environment. Dust is an ever-present problem; sealed cases and frequent cleaning of cameras, lenses and film holders is imperative. Heat effects on sensitive materials may be minimized by using insulated cases. and having all cases painted white. Keep film holders and lenses in plastic bags.

32. Rocks and Wind Clouds, California. Further expansion of contrast would misinter-pret the basic mood of the delicate wind clouds. The G filter was used, with less than normal negative development.

CLOUDS

In their most dramatic or most delicate forms, clouds universally arouse a definite emotional response in the spectator. Consequently, no phenomenon of the natural world has been more widely photographed—and none has caused more perplexity to the photographer. Various rule-of-thumb instructions for the use of filters in recording clouds have been published, but no adequate interpretation is possible unless each subject is analyzed individually and the print is thoroughly visualized. The ordinary approach to photography of cloudscapes results in an image in which the blue sky is usually far too dark and the sunlit portions of the clouds are a formless white. As in other subjects, the photographer should make some analysis of the actual values of the clouds, not only in themselves, but in relation to the general landscape, blue sky, and objects rising against them.

First, the range of values between clouds and sky should be considered. The intensity of the average sky is about 300 to 400 candles per square foot; a deep north-zenith sky in high altitudes registers about 200 c.p.sq.ft.; sky values near the horizon may be very high—800 c.p.sq.ft. or more. The brightness of massive sunlit clouds ranges from approximately 400 to 1,600 c.p.sq.ft., or higher. It is safe to assume that the difference between average blue sky and ordinary summer clouds does not exceed 1:3 in range, though massive clouds such as thunderheads may have a greater range, while their shadowed portions will usually approximate the deeper sky tone. On orthochromatic film the sky is rendered approximately one zone higher than on panchromatic film, and the contrast between sky and clouds is consequently less. Assuming that panchromatic film is used and the scale of sky and cloud brightness is 1:3 or 1:4, it is easy to see how an "average" exposure and normal development may produce an effect that is quite flat and unrelated to the emotional quality of the subject itself. Even a 1:8 range does not have a great emotional impact.

Think of the placement of sky and cloud brightnesses on the symbolic gray scale, where such a relationship would represent *literal* placement on Zone V and Zone VIII. To expose for this normal placement and increase development, while it might add contrast to other areas of the image, would not favor the higher values of the clouds. Attempting to print this negative deeper in tone must inevitably result in slightly flattened high values. Reducing the exposure placements to Zones IV and VII and giving a considerable amount of development may yield an image of increased emotional impact, but the difficulty will then lie in preserving the illusion of light, for if the sky is too dark, there is a false balance of tone.

The use of high-contrast filters darkens the sky to a marked degree, yet unless the exposure is kept within certain limits the whites of the clouds are almost certain to "block," and so lose their appearance of delicate translucency. No sensitive photographer is satisfied with such chalky tones in place of lucid brilliance. Except under unusual conditions, the photography of clouds and sky seldom requires a heavier filter than a Wratten K2 or a No. 12, and placement of values on the exposure scale when such a filter is used should be within one zone of normal. To lower the placement two zones and *then* add a filter would result in a distressingly dark sky and undue exaggeration within the cloud. The following table is an *approximate* guide to placements of average cloud and sky effects, exclusive of massive storm clouds, which are treated in the next section.

Sky Intensity (north-zenith)	Cloud Type	Cloud Brightness	Zonal placement. Sky	Clouds	Filter	Development
200 c.p.sq.ft.	High cirrus or wind	600-800 c.p.sq.ft.	V	VII	K-1	1 zone expansion
"	High cirrus or wind	600-800 c.p.sq.ft.	V	VII	K2 or XI	normal
"	Ordinary nimbus	Approximately 1000 c.p.sq.ft.	IV	VI to VII	K1	1 zone expansion
"	Ordinary nimbus	Approximately 1000 c.p.sq.ft.	V	VII to VIII	K2	normal
"	Brilliant cumulus	Approximately 1600 c.p.sq.ft.	IV	VII plus	K1	1 zone expansion
"	Brilliant cumulus	Approximately 1600 c.p.sq.ft.	V	VIII plus	K2	normal

The above is but a rough approximation and must be varied if the sky is of other than average intensity. Remember that the filter will slightly clarify the values *within* the cloud, as it removes atmospheric haze and strengthens the shadows in the cloud masses. Above all, do not attempt to create the illusion of radiance by producing an effect of harsh contrast. The use of the Wratten No. 12 filter is preferred by many; it will give slightly higher contrast than the K2, but not as much as the G. The G and A filters yield much higher contrast than the K2 and No. 12, but will be helpful on hazy days and when the sky is slightly grayed by water vapor. (Smoke haze, being on the yellowish side *in the sky* will be rendered *lighter* by a strong filter, although smoke haze may appear bluish—and react thus to filters—when seen against distant landscape.)

The sky near the horizon is considerably brighter than the sky at the zenith, so that sky-cloud separation there will be more difficult to retain. Furthermore, the angle of the sun in relation to cloud forms makes a marked difference in their brightness. Clouds that are opposite the sun in the early morning or the late afternoon are of comparatively high brilliancy but possess a minimum modulation of values. At about 45° to the sun the clouds reveal their form to the fullest extent. As the angle lessens they develop increasingly brilliant edges of light, and finally become extremely contrasty (when they pass in front of the sun). The blaze of this acutely sunlit edge can rise to thousands of candles per square foot; it may be visualized in the print as a pure white, and in order to accentuate fully its dramatic intensity, other values of the image may be printed considerably darker than normal.

At this point the reader is reminded that it is very difficult to measure the brightness of clouds with any degree of accuracy with ordinary meters. You can arrive at an approximation, after processing, by comparing on a densitometer the high opacities of the negative with the opacities of your test negatives (see Book 2). This, of course, does not help the particular picture at hand—but it would be helpful for future reference. In the field, the surrounding sky can be evaluated and—if the foreground values (if any) have adequate brightness—this sky value can be placed on Zone V. The bright sunlit clouds will probably fall within the exposure scale. A reading of the general scene will probably suggest too short an exposure. It is here that a sensitive exposure photometer such as the S.E.I. meter is invaluable; brilliantly illuminated clouds with brightnesses up to 2400 c.p.sq.ft. can be measured directly at the time of exposure, and within a very small field of view. The brilliant edges of back-lighted clouds show both reflected brightness and transmitted intensity—and are therefore far brighter than the most brilliant thunderheads illuminated by flat or side lighting.

Very early in the morning or late in the evening the predominance of red and yellow light has its effect on the image scale. Only in rare instances does the sky near the horizon appear dominantly bluish under such conditions. The use of K2, G, and A filters may only cancel the effect desired, as the yellow and red components of the sky are elevated in value at the same time that the blue is lowered. Under such conditions, where a general saturation of color infuses both sky and clouds, the use of a green filter is indicated; with this filter place the values fairly low in the scale, with attendant full development.

With poor handling, the substance of the cloud can easily be distorted into either a chalky, formless mass or a dead, gray substance of plaster-of-Paris quality. The rich, massive opalescence of cloud substance depends upon moderate exaggeration of values.

If landscape and clouds are to be photographed together, the problem is vastly complicated. Except in open scenes with fairly flat light, you are confronted with a full scale that you cannot expect to hold in its entirety; yet a major distortion of any important value may destroy the illusion of light. For example, a landscape containing summer clouds, brilliant and full of light, may possess certain areas of shadow that will conflict with the tonal balance of the sky if rendered too dark through exposure for the bright areas alone. In spite of the necessity for adequate interpretation of the whites in cloud forms, once you accept a shadow value as an essential part of the picture you must base your exposure on it, and do as best you can to retain the higher values.

It is almost certain that an average meter reading of a landscape with clouds will place the shadows of near objects on or below the threshold of the negative. For example, in a typical mountain landscape the meter readings were 25 for the shadow on a near rock, 100 for the foliage, 400 for the sky, and 800 to 1,600 for the clouds. With normal placement plus a K2 filter, and normal development, the shadows would have had that bugaboo lunar quality; it was necessary to make some compensations to hold the values of the entire scene within reasonable limits. Placement of the shadows on Zone IV would raise the values of sky and clouds and require a somewhat reduced development time. With a moderately strong filter the shadows (placed on Zone III) would effectively revert to a Zone II placement, though the sky and clouds would be adequately separated. With a K2 filter, shadows placed on Zone IV would revert to Zone III. A compromise can be effected by 1) employing the water-bath or the two-solution method of development, or 2) employing a weak filter and giving normal development. Either will give a fairly full-bodied negative without seriously lowering the shadow tones. In fact, the shadows may benefit slightly from the general lens and camera flare. It may be rather difficult to print such a negative by ordinary means, but with the use of a water-bath print developer, as outlined in Book 3, p. 49, the extreme range can be satisfactorily controlled.

Perhaps the best way to handle a subject of this type is to use a polarizer, providing the sky areas are at the proper angle of 90° to the sun (see page 32). The polarizer will lower the value of the sky and slightly clear the atmospheric-haze effect, yet will not depreciate the shadow value of near objects. The negative, being slightly softer when made through a polarizer, may require a small increase of development time.

When a landscape with clouds is photographed more or less into the sun, a large proportion of foreground is shadow, and if the illusion of light is to be preserved, the shadows should be rendered in darker tones than in the example mentioned above. The cloud values, being extremely brilliant, imply less-than-normal development to control the brightness range; however, I caution you to proceed with care, as the very brilliant cloud edges must be rendered in the print as white and therefore should be of adequate high opacity in the negative.

So far, clouds under reasonably clear conditions and in skies of average intensity have been considered. When the sky is a very intense blue, the whole problem is simplified, but when it is unusually light, or there is a prevalence of mist or haze, another set of problems bedevils the photographer. A scene including both high clouds and morning mist, for example, can be photographed only by placing the values fairly high on the scale, giving rather full development, and printing with the utmost care to preserve the high opalescent values. Along the seacoast, masses of sunlit fog may have high brightness but lack strong internal form, and it is difficult to avoid a dead, flat quality in the print. As in the photography of snow in shade, or of great storm clouds, the negative should be rich and massive in quality. The illusion of brilliance is supported by the inclusion of small bits of landscape—trees or other objects—that are rendered very dark.

It must be emphasized that an image of mere high contrast may completely fail to interpret the luminosity of sunlit vapor and clouds. Other subjects in nature present similar problems. The mist from hot springs, the smoke from fires, and the industrial haze of cities all require massive negative quality; a low-density negative will usually yield an image of abrupt, coarse values.

When you are photographing heads or other close objects against a sky containing clouds, your visualization must include awareness of the background definition. In all images except those made with lenses of very short focus the depth of field may not be adequate to give a pleasing definition to clouds. High wind clouds, if unsharp, may appear as actual defects in the negative, and stronger cloud forms give a confused, shapeless background. There are only two solutions to this problem. One is to throw the background completely out of focus, and the second is to work at a distance from the principle subject that will admit of adequate depth of field. See page 82 on portraiture for further elaboration.

Clouds, of course, are usually in motion; but occasionally the photographer, for lack of a static reference point, may fail to observe their movement visually, with the result that exposures as short as $\frac{1}{5}$ second may show motion in the clouds. The cloud edge should be rendered with sharpness, unless the mood of swift driving wind and scudding clouds demands some evidence of movement (as with water).

It is within the province of this text to remind you that the direction of cloud motion must be taken into consideration so that the cloud forms are properly "placed" in the picture area, just as other moving objects are adjusted to an appropriate space. Also, since clouds often move swiftly across the camera's field of view, the time lag between composing and exposing may result in a major change of position unless the direction of their movement is anticipated. A reflex camera is ideal for cloud photography.

In large cloud forms, parts of the mass are shadowed, and these areas sometimes equal in effective brightness the values of the sky. This can result in a poor separation of values in a sky-and-cloud composition. For the same reason, in photographing architecture against cloudy skies, the separation of the building surfaces must be considered not only in relation to blue sky, but in relation to shadowed cloud values as well. Further, it is seldom that any building surface is as brilliant as a brightly sunlit cloud. In visualizing such images, it may be advisable to wait until values of near objects are in satisfactory opposition to those of the clouds.

Storm Clouds

Storm clouds are, as a rule, of lower brightness than what may be called average summer clouds. Not only is the actual brightness lower, but the brightness range is shorter. Yet in order to achieve the emotional impact of storm clouds you must visualize the print as encompassing a full, vibrant scale from black to white. The first step is to check on the extremes of values; if there are white, rolling thunderclouds, you must be certain that they are not rendered either blank white or in dingy gray tonalities. As in the photography of snow in shade, negatives of smooth, rich storm clouds must have *body;* that is, they must be of sufficient density to hold a solid, nongranular tone in the print. Snow in shade *appears* quite light, while its actual brightness* may be low. The darker tonalities of storm clouds can also fool you, for they may often be considerably brighter than shaded snow, although in comparison with the sunlit clouds they may appear somber and ponderous. In recent tests, a typical overcast preceding a thunderstorm gave an average reading of 400 c.p.sq.ft., whereas a snowbank in shade, exposed to the open blue sky, registered only 100 c.p.sq.ft. Yet to casual recollection the snowbank was "brighter." The solution, instead of the customary one of placing the dark cloud areas at the bottom of the exposure scale, is to give ample placement in Zones IV or V, providing, of course, that the sunlit areas are not placed above Zone VIII (without special developing procedures).

Occasionally in thunderstorms the overcast will open and allow a tremendous amount of reflected light to illuminate the subject from a large rolling thunderhead in full sun. This "storm light" being reflected from a white cloud surface will approximate the mean color temperature of daylight, as it is more or less a direct reflection and not a scattering of light through continuous cloud.

More frequently with storm clouds, however, there is no brilliant dominating sunlit area, but rather a subtle variation of rich grays, the tonalities of which seldom exceed 1:4 in range. The problem is not one of creating extraordinary contrast, but of obtaining an image scale that equals or exceeds the scale of the subject while still retaining a full-bodied negative. If the same values are encountered in textured wood or rock, they might well be placed low on the scale, with full separation achieved by prolonged development. In this case the eyes do not mind the textural exaggeration. But in the case of smooth, continuous-textured clouds, the values should be placed fairly high in the scale and given a rather full development. It is perfectly possible to place the overcast on Zones IV or V, as suggested, and develop to a rather high degree, without blocking any of the values. Should small edges of sunlit clouds appear, their emotional effect usually justifies their rendition as pure white. If there are large areas of extremely bright masses, of course the problem changes, as a loss of texture and tonal gradation in them can be very disturbing.

High-contrast filters have little effect on a continuous, gray-toned storm-cloud sky. A K2 is about as powerful a filter as should be used, since all that filters of this type can do is to clarify the haze between spectator and clouds and slightly deepen those cloud areas which are illuminated with reflected blue light. Striking effects can be obtained with strong filters only at sunrise or sunset, when the color of the high open sky is definitely bluish. However, before attempting dramatic exaggerations, you should always give thought to conveying a sense of light and delicate substance, since cloud forms rendered with too much contrast have a brutality and a harshness that are in no way consistent with their real appearance and substance.

---

* In this same light, ordinary asphalt pavement registered 100 c.p.sq.ft. and yellowish-green foliage 50 c.p.sq.ft., about one-half its value in bright direct sunlight.

33. Moonrise, Half Dome, Yosemite (from *Yosemite and the Sierra Nevada,* Houghton Mifflin Co.). Late afternoon light on mountain. Cliff values about 200 c.p.sq.ft. Moon's brightness somewhat less than brightness of snow. Moon value placed on about Zone VI. Expanded development.

THE MOON AND MOONLIGHT

Inclusion of the moon in an exterior scene is a rather simple problem, but certain facts must be borne in mind, as follows:

1. The moon subtends 30′ ($\frac{1}{2}$°) of arc and will not appear very large in the photograph unless a lens of rather long focus is used or considerable enlargement is given the negative. With a 6-inch lens it will appear only about $\frac{1}{20}$ inch in diameter! With a 24-inch lens it will appear about $\frac{1}{5}$ inch in diameter.

2. The moon moves about $\frac{1}{8}$ of its diameter in 15 seconds; hence exposures should be *less* than 15 seconds if apparent distortion is to be avoided. For very large images of the moon, say $\frac{1}{2}$ inch in diameter, the exposure should not be more than 5 seconds; even this will show a slight movement.

3. The moon has a surface of (presumably!) volcanic ash, of about the same reflectivity as the Nevada desert ranges as seen from the air. For practical purposes the average brightness of the moon, as it appears from sea level, is about 250 c.p.sq.ft. Certain areas of the moon are slightly brighter, and its surface when seen in crescent is brighter than when the moon is full. At high elevations, where there is less atmosphere between the observer and the satellite, the effective brightness of the moon will exceed 250 c.p.sq.ft. The brightness of the

moon in daylight (such as when it is rising a day or so before full moon) is greater than when it is shining in the night sky—all appearances notwithstanding! To the brightness of the moon you must add the brightness of the sky. The atmosphere absorbs moonlight about the same both at night and day, but in daylight the atmosphere is illuminated by the sun and its brightness is *added* to that of the moon. Hence the brightness of the rising moon about an hour before sundown may be around 300 c.p.sq.ft. (the brightness of the sky would be about 100 c.p.sq.ft.) At the zenith the moon's brightness may exceed 300 c.p.sq.ft.

4. Visualizing the placement of the moon on the exposure scale must be on an emotional rather than a factual basis. Emotionally the moon is a "shining" object, and its brightness must be suggested in the print. Hence when the moon is included in a sunlit or a twilight landscape, it will have a value of about Zone VII or slightly higher. This placement will preserve the details of the moon's surface. If only an impression of brightness is required, it can be placed on Zone VIII or higher. Of course, the tonalities of the other parts of the image will have a profound effect on the mood of the picture as a whole. You are safe in placing the moon on Zone VII or a little higher. If you have a meter such as the S.E.I., you can measure the brightness of the moon directly, but you can also estimate the actual brightness of the moon by measuring the brightness of the sky near the moon and adding 250 c.p.sq.ft. to your results.

5. It is important to remember that when you use a filter to deepen the value of the sky around the moon, you are also lowering the effective brightness of the moon. A strong filter such as the G might reduce the brightness of the sky to about one-third its unfiltered value. If the sky measured about 100 c.p.sq.ft., you would assume the effective brightness of the moon to be about 285 c.p.sq.ft. This must be taken into consideration when placing the effective brightness of the moon on the exposure scale.

6. At twilight, the foreground may be of very low brightness, and the brightness range of foreground to moon be beyond the exposure scale of the film. In such cases the *average foreground* should not be placed below Zone III (Zone II if definition is not vital) and development of the negative should be adjusted to the moon's position on the scale. For example, if a twilight landscape foreground measures 1.6 c.p.sq.ft. and is placed on Zone III, the moon (now slightly above 250 c.p.sq.ft., as the sky would be rather dark) will fall on Zone X. This requires a water-bath development, or, better, development by the two-solution process (see page 78). With a K2 filter (using a factor of 3, because of the strong bluish quality of the sky) the exposure would be 1 second at f/16 with a film of an exposure index of 100.

Photographing *by* moonlight is something quite different from photographing by daylight with the moon included in the picture. The intensity of moonlight is very low; the reciprocity effect must be accounted for in all calculations. When we mention a "lunar" effect in general photography, we imply black, empty shadows and relatively harsh high values. Of course the inherent reflectivity of materials is the same under moonlight as under sunlight. (The spectrum is almost the same, but the material of the moon's surface reflects only about 25% of the light falling on it.) The intensity of moonlight reaching the earth is about 400,000 times weaker than sunlight. While the illuminated and shadowed areas of the subject bear the same relationship to each other as under sunlight, the shadows are of such low brightness that the normal eye cannot perceive detail within them (the threshold of vision is not overcome). To create "Moonlight" effects in sunlight, we place the brightness of the deep shadowed areas on or below Zone I and develop for a negative of considerable contrast (augmented by the use of a G or A filter.)

Many rule-of-thumb statements have been made as to the correct exposure for moonlight scenes; that is, scenes illuminated by moonlight. It is quite impossible to make a sensible rule, for the simple reason that as exposure is prolonged, the moonlight effect gradually blends into a daylight effect. An exposure of five or six hours by moonlight will give an effect of rather flat daylight, with indefinite edges (as the moon traverses the sky both shadow edges and highlights move with it), and rather bleak shadows. Obviously, there is no reason to imitate daylight with moonlight! But just what values moonlit objects should have to give the impression of moonlight depends upon personal visualization. I personally feel that what would be a flat surface of Zone V value in daylight should be rendered about Zone III in moonlight, and that lower values should be rendered black. Values higher than Zone V in daylight should be rendered about two zones lower in moonlight. But sharp highlights, such as reflections from metal or water, should be rendered as pure white, since this quality of "glimmer" is integral with the impression of moonlight.

Just how are you to go about calculating the proper exposure for moonlight scenes? Begin by establishing an exposure value for a Zone V placement in sunlight; light-gray rock, a conventional gray card, etc., can be used. A Zone V value in *sunlight* represents a reflectivity of about 18%, and a brightness of about 200 c.p.sq.ft. The exposure for a Zone V placement on the exposure scale with a film of 64 ASA exposure index would be 1/200 sec. at f/8, or 1/800 sec. at f/4.

Considering that moonlight is about $\frac{1}{400,000}$ as bright as sunlight, the exposure will be 8 minutes at f/4. But if you wish to place this Zone V brightness on Zone III, the exposure will be as little as 2 minutes. *However*, the reciprocity effect (see Book 2, p. 13) would be from 2x to 4x at least, depending upon the film used and the actual exposure time given (you might want to use a smaller lens stop—f/8, for example, which would require a basic exposure of about 8 minutes). So your 2-minute exposure at f/4 would be actually 4, 6, or 8 (or more) minutes, depending upon the degree of reciprocity effect involved. The simple formula would then be:

Zone V Exposure in Sunlight x 400,000 x ½ or ¼ for lower zonal placement x 2 or more for reciprocity effect = exposure in moonlight

The most valuable suggestion I can give is: Make a test for yourself, because you probably have a definite impression in your mind of how a moonlit scene should appear! The above information will aid you in determining your own procedures. It is better to start from a logical demonstrative approach than to attack the problem on a purely empirical basis.

I wish to acknowledge with thanks some of the above factual data received from the U. S. Naval Observatory, Washington, D. C.

NATURALISTIC DETAILS

Photography is very well adapted to the rendition of textures and complex detail. The nostalgic quality of old wood, objects of rich patina, minute patterns of natural shape—all these respond to the searching clarity of the lens. Of all the arts, photography encourages exploration of the minutiae, and in fact is often more convincing in its interpretation of objects of intimate environment than in that of the vaster aspects of nature.

Frequently students and practicing photographers automatically categorize the many aspects of the medium into "possible," "difficult," and—too often— "impossible," and thereby limit their experience and pleasure in their work to narrow channels of subject and style. The differences lie far less in the photographic techniques than in control of the subject itself; for example, "fashion photography" presents problems that relate to clothes, settings, and dramatic lightings far more complex than the problems of the camera and the laboratory. To make good photographs of skiing demands a good knowledge of the sport itself; the actual photographic techniques are closely allied to those of general snow photography. While the same general *principles* of exposure and development relate to a photograph of a distant mountain and a small leaf form, the camera requirements are quite different; the mountain can be photographed with a fixed-focus camera, while the leaf form demands a camera of long bellows extension, ground-glass focusing, and firm tripod equipment. The skiing photograph demands a flexible small instrument with a rapid shutter. These differences are not as profound as the inherent differences of the subjects themselves. It is of vital importance that you recognize this—that you use caution in venturing into the domain of special subjects, but that you do not restrict yourself in the application of straightforward photographic techniques to the tremendous variety of subject matter at your command.

For photographs for "decorative" use — that is, material for overmantels, screens, etc. — an unlimited wealth of subject matter lies in the world of leaves, shore details, ice crystals, mineral forms, etc. I am not referring to subject matter requiring high magnification, but to those things which can be photographed with regular field equipment.

Control of depth of field by camera swings and tilts (see Book 1) and the use of small lens stops will be found necessary in photographing the greater number of small objects. Focusing is critical; if possible, focus with the lens set at the stop to be used (after composing and roughly focusing with the lens wide-open). Wind movements, camera vibration, depth of field, etc. are all exaggerated with large images of small objects. Brightness values may be hard to determine, and the near presence of the camera and the operator may interfere with the light falling upon the subjects from the sky. (It is obvious that anything interrupting sunlight is easily seen, but a general reduction of skylight may not be very apparent to you, yet may seriously reduce the brightness of the subject.) Watch for "bellows sag" at long camera extensions, and do not fail to calculate the extension factor for proper exposure: A 2x focal-length extension requires a 4x exposure (refer to Book 1).

34. House, Late Evening, Yosemite. Made with a Hasselblad camera, 135mm lens at f/4. Brightness of side of building placed on Zone IV, illuminated window brightness about Zone XII. Negative developed in the two-solution developer (p. 78).

THE MINIATURE CAMERA OUT OF DOORS

I subscribe to the general professional opinion that miniature cameras (especially the 35mm instruments) are not ideal for landscape work. The images of distant mountains, for example, never seem adequately sharp. Perhaps this is due to some inherent difficulty of optical corrections of the lens, or to some complex psychological reaction to tonal values and the inevitable negative grain. In any event, with the 35mm cameras images of distant objects are never as precise and satisfying as are those made with large instruments. However, landscapes made with 2¼x2¼ and 2¼x3¼ cameras are much more satisfactory. Perhaps the greater degree of enlargement necessary with the 35mm negatives has much to do with it.

But fortunately landscape is only one phase of photography out of doors. Before dismissing it, consider a few of the technical details that are essential to satisfactory results with the miniature camera in this field:

1. Avoid high density in negatives of distant landscape.

2. Do not overdevelop (in fact, less-than-normal development will give smoother results with less grain).

3. Achieve contrast by oblique lighting and the use of moderately strong filters (and of printing papers of higher-than-normal contrast). Do *not* attempt to gain contrast by reducing exposure and increasing time of development!

4. Use a lens of as long focus as possible for distant subjects. Select a film of minimum emulsion thickness. Use a developer that favors "surface development" (see Book 2). Use gelatin filters or glass filters of the highest optical quality.

These suggestions apply, of course, to all phases of miniature-camera work, but they are especially applicable to distant landscape, city scapes, etc.

For most outdoor subjects in natural light the miniature camera will be found a most versatile and useful instrument. It should never be pressed beyond its logical limitations. In small negatives the "chemical" quality of the image is exaggerated in broad smooth areas of tone, such as the sky, in which negative grain and minute defects are most clearly revealed. Obviously "fine-grain" images are required, although a coarser grain may be permissible in near objects of complex texture. Exposure and development must be carried out within relatively close tolerances, as explained in Book 2 (pp. 88-90) because increase of development time will have a definite effect on negative grain. Also, there is a practical limit to the maximum opacity of the miniature negative, since for various reasons it should be enlarged through a condenser-type enlarger in which the Callier effect (see Book 2 [p. 24] and Book 3 [p. 21]) is more pronounced than it is with the enlargement of negatives of normal size by diffuse light. It is therefore necessary to work for negatives of relatively low contrast for use in condenser-type enlargers. In reference to my zone system, this would mean that the optimum negative density for Zone VI value would be about 0.8 or 0.9 above film-base-fog density, or its arithmetical equivalent, an opacity of 6.3 or 8.0 above film-base-fog opacity.

With this limitation in mind, values should be placed on the exposure scale *in consideration for the development of the negative*, whereas in ordinary photography development can usually be determined by the position of the high values of the subject on the exposure scale. It is better to work for a fairly thin and soft negative, with special emphasis on adequate exposure of the essential shadow values. Recourse to papers of higher-than-normal contrast may be required. Referring to Book 3 (pp. 45-50) you will see that extensive control of contrast is possible with any given grade of paper by the use of various developers, and by certain controls in the print-developing process. Consider the enormous amount of miniature-camera work that evidences the "soot-and-chalk" quality, chiefly due to original underexposure of shadows and gross "blocking" of high values. In such cases, no selection of paper will be of much help, as the defect lies within the negative itself.

In miniature-camera work, no matter how perfect the lens, how fine the resolution of the film, or what fine grain the developer may yield, you must recognize the limits of resolution of lens and film, and accept the fact that minute subject textures cannot be as finely interpreted in an enlargement from a 35mm negative as in a contact print from a 4x5 or an 8x10 negative. Considerable disappointment results from 35mm photography of foam, sand, delicately textured skin, etc., the refined textures of which approach the resolving power of the miniature-negative emulsion. Such subject details are rendered very small indeed in the image of a 50mm lens. They may be entirely lost in the negative emulsion, and this loss is quite apparent when the film is enlarged to any considerable extent. On the other hand, a 10-inch lens renders an image about 5x as large as does a 50mm (2-inch) lens, and in a contact print or a moderate enlargement these minute details are retained. Hence in visualizing images to be made with small cameras, emphasis should be placed on broad forms, definite textures, and decisive edges rather than on subtle, minute textures and tonalities.

While most exposures should be planned so that the standardized development procedure can be applied, it is at times possible to vary the development for special purposes. Often a series of photographs is made of one subject, or in an environment of consistent quality. For instance, in photographing street scenes you can assume that the quality of all the images in any one location will be fairly consistent, and you therefore proceed to evaluate essential shadow and highlight values, place them on the exposure scale as you require, and then make many photographs in the same locale without further calculations. Accordingly, if one roll contains only images of similar subjects with similar exposures, it can be developed in relation to that one set of circumstances, within the following limits: A slight increase of normal developing time is permissible, especially if the negatives do not have large areas of smooth middle-tone values, and are not to be greatly enlarged.

a. With soft lighting, development time can be $1\frac{1}{4}$ normal without producing excessive grain (providing your "normal" represents a fairly low contrast range).

b. With harsh lighting, the developing time can be reduced to about $\frac{3}{4}$ normal developing time without losing "body" in the shadows.

c. When much less than normal developing time is used to compensate for very high subject contrast, the middle tones and the shadows may be seriously weakened in value and the resulting prints flat and "muddy."

For control of excessively harsh values I recommend the use of the following two-solution developer (which was not available to me when the first printing of Book 2 was issued).

TWO-SOLUTION DEVELOPER

Solution I	Elon-(Metol)	7.5 grams
	Sodium Sulfite des.	100 grams
	Water to make	1 liter
Solution II	1 to 10% Kodalk (10 to 100 grams per liter)	

Immerse negative in Solution I for a period of time determined by the placement of the highest brightness on the exposure scale, then immerse in Solution II for at least 3 minutes.*

A 1% solution of Borax will perhaps give slightly finer grain, and therefore is advisable with small film. The immersion time in the Kodalk or Borax solution is the same.

SUGGESTED DEVELOPING TIME FOR TWO-SOLUTION DEVELOPER

Super-XX roll film (ASA film speed 125). Solutions at 68°F.

Zone VI Controls (for condenser enlargers). Zone VI brightness placed on various higher zones, but developed to retain density of 0.9 above film-base-fog density in every case.

	Solution 1	Solution 2
Zone VI brightness on Zone VI (normal)	7 min.	3 min.
Zone VII (N-1)	4½ min.	3 min.
Zone VIII (N-2)	3½ min.	3 min.
Zone IX (N-3)	2½ min.	3 min.
Zone X (N-4)	1¾ min.	3 min.

Zone VIII Controls (for condenser enlargers). Zone VIII brightness placed on various higher zones, but developed to retain density of 1.35 above film-base-fog density in every case.

	Solution 1	Solution 2
Zone VIII brightness on Zone VIII (normal)	7 min.	3 min.
Zone IX (N-1)	4¾ min.	3 min.
Zone X (N-2)	4 min.	3 min.
Zone XI (N-3)	3⅓ min.	3 min.
Zone XII (N-4)	2¾ min.	3 min.
Zone XIII (N-5)	2 min.	3 min.

Constant agitation in both solutions important

Threshold (Zone I) density drops very little more with 1¾- and 2-minute developing times than with the "Normal" developing times.

NOTE: This formula is superior to the two-solution formula appearing in the first printing of Book 2.

With this process, place the important shadow brightnesses well within the exposure scale; place Zones I, II, and III values as you would with normal exposure and development. With the shortest developing times (N-4 and N-5) it may be advisable to place the lowest values one Zone higher on the scale. This, of course, raises the placement of the higher zones, but the very short developing times will control them adequately.

When photographing with a larger camera—say a 4x5 view camera—you see the image on the ground glass and you can evaluate compositional elements and image details far better than you can through the conventional finders of the small instruments. Hence I strongly urge the use of large cutout cards (Book 1, p. 5) through which the subject is seen with full visual clarity. These are useful in all kinds of photography, suggesting composition and scale.

For action, or when the camera is held in the hand, the regular finders must suffice. As pointed out early in this series, you must learn to *project* the confines of your image upon the subject; you must be aware of countless details of form,

*I am indebted to Mr. Frederick Quandt, of the Photography Department of the California School of Fine Arts, San Francisco, for the up-to-date control table above.

color, and texture, and it is difficult to appreciate these elements when the subject is viewed through the usual small finder.

In Book 1 of this series *(Camera & Lens)* I strongly advised the practice of "dry shooting"—that is, going through all the calculations and operations of making a photograph, but not actually exposing a negative. I feel this is of great value with the miniature camera. Facility with the instrument is of the greatest importance; the hands must instinctively *know* the various controls.

As the miniature camera is an instrument of *immediacy* in the larger part of its applications, there is not much opportunity to organize perfectly planned and visualized photographs. In the excitement of working with the camera, new angles of view may be used without consideration for changed light values and directions; sheer forgetfulness of shutter and lens settings are all too frequent, and appropriate shutter speeds for moving objects may be wrongly calculated. In approaching any general subject, such as a sports event, beach activity, mountain climbing, it will be well to think first of all of the possible problems that may evolve, and determine the exposures in relation to three angles of light: 1) light back of the camera, 2) at around 90° to lens axis, and 3) back of the subject. As a rule the rough estimate of the exposure values of these lightings would be 1, $\frac{1}{2}$ and $\frac{1}{4}$. or an inclusive difference of three stops. A little planning and a little practice are always worth the effort.

See the LEICA MANUAL by Willard D. Morgan, Morgan & Morgan, Inc., for a tremendous amount of valuable factual information on the operation and the application of the miniature camera.

With cameras such as the Rolleiflex and the Hasselblad and other $2\frac{1}{4}$x$2\frac{1}{4}$ instruments we have somewhat less flexibility than with the 35mm cameras, but more control in operation and negative development. We are not so concerned with the problems of grain as the enlargements are, as a rule, only half as great as from 35mm negatives. But great care and precision in operation are required in order to achieve the maximum results possible with these instruments. In using reflex cameras in the conventional way, the axis of the lens is lower than the normal position of the eye; this makes a considerable difference in the positioning and aspect of the near subjects compared to that obtained by the eye-level cameras. Reflex cameras can be held at eye level, or even held high overhead for the desired effects. The new "pentaprism" finders are superior in every respect, as they give eye-level images, right-side up and right-side to. At this time, these finders are available only with the 35mm reflex-type cameras. "Sports-finder" attachments permit the use of reflex cameras at eye level, but are independent of the focusing mechanisms (range-finder, or ground-glass systems.)

Of all these cameras the single-lens reflex is perhaps the most satisfactory, especially as there is no problem of parallax. The Hasselblad, with its interchangeable lenses and roll film backs is, to my knowledge, the most versatile camera of its type. But you must recognize the fact that there is no single camera that is capable of *everything*. Your problem is to select the cameras and lenses that are most efficient in relation to the requirements of your own work. I find it difficult to imagine Henri Cartier-Bresson using anything but a 35mm—or Edward Weston using anything but a large view camera. One man will prefer a Leica, another a Contax; one will use a Rolleiflex, another a Hasselblad. The physique, temperament, and objectives of the photographer determine the instruments of his choice.

35. Spider in Window, Cape Cod. A good example of the efficacy of alternate water-bath development (see Book 2, p. 104). The values within (the picture was made in a building, looking out to a near-by board fence) were about 0.4 c.p.sq.ft. The brightness of the outside fence was about 100 c.p.sq.ft. Development favored the lowest tones (they were placed on Zone I) and reduced the value of the fence to Zones VII-VIII.

PORTRAITURE

Perception of the form of objects is both tactile and visual. With artificial light, the lighting is applied in relation to the form of the subject, for, as is shown in Book 5, the total artificial illumination on an object can be built up from many indirect sources in various positions. In natural light the form can be clarified and accentuated by proper orientation of the subject to the basically uncontrollable light. With the three main types of natural light—sunlight, skylight, and shielded light (natural indoor light from windows, doorways, and skylights)—countless variations are encountered.

Sunlight is the most difficult natural light source for portraiture because of its sharply defined directional quality combined with relatively deep shadows. It is perhaps most satisfactory very early or very late in the day, when the sun's rays are closer to parallel with the axis of the lens. In fact, axis sunlight is to my mind the most luminous and revealing light of all. While true axis sunlight can never be obtained without projecting the shadow of the camera or the operator on the subject, it is possible, through slight displacement of camera position from true axis, to achieve a virtual axis light (see page 7). The greater the focal length of the lens (and therefore the greater the distance between camera and subject), the less this displacement need be. The shift is ordinarily to one side of the subject, though occasionally, for certain striking images, it may be to a position below. However, there are relatively few portrait subjects who appreciate the uncompromising revelations of direct sunlight, and its strong shadow effects. Also, the tendency of the sitter to squint must be considered. Some people can tolerate much more direct sunlight in the eyes than can others. Eye fatigue and less-than-normal hours of sleep contribute to the tendency to squint in direct sunlight. Also, in bright sunlight the size of the pupil of the eye is considerably reduced, and this will be apparent in the image.

The best background for heads in sunlight is, to my mind, the open sky. Normally, the brightness of sunlit skin may be placed on Zone VI (or sometimes Zone V, with appropriate development); shadows then appear quite deep in tone. There should be little difficulty in separating skin tones from sky tones, especially if a mild filter, such as a K1, is employed. If skin brightness is placed higher on the scale, say on Zone VII, the shadow values (around Zone IV and V) may merge with the sky values, or if the complexion is rather dark; the sunlit portions also may come too close to the sky values. Then the use of a K2 filter is helpful, although with it there is the possibility of creating a pasty or milky skin tone with panchromatic film.

Sky values are variable; the open sky of high altitudes and desert regions is much deeper than the open sky of cities, and the photographer must make tests in his environment to establish the proper exposure and filter applications. The sky progresses in tone from light to dark as the angle of view elevates from horizon to zenith. With lenses of relatively short focal lengths this progression of tones produces an interesting background effect—a feeling of space is achieved.

Other effective backgrounds are foliage and smooth surfaces. Foliage can be confusing. We must watch for unwanted shadows appearing on smooth backgrounds. An open door or window may be used as a black background. Here, though, care must be taken to keep dark hair from merging with dark background. A very satisfying arrangement for portraiture in sun is shown in Figure 36a, where a head in sunlight is taken against an open doorway, with portions of the door frame used as compositional elements.

One of the chief problems in using sunlight for portraits is control of the shadows caused by hats or visors, or—with deep-set eyes—preservation of the luminosity of the eye itself. The practical solution is a very low sun and a fairly low camera viewpoint, but it must be remembered that a low camera viewpoint emphasizes the lower part of the face and may often prove highly unsatisfactory. The use of reflectors is justifiable if no false lighting effects result. Reflectors of high specular quality (such as metal or crinkled aluminum foil) inevitably produce both secondary highlights and shadows that negate the illusion of normal shadow light from the sky. The best reflector of all is a broad, chalk-white board or some white fabric large enough to throw an enveloping light over the entire subject.

To preserve an illusion of sunlight when light is not intense and shadows are not pronounced, try a ratio of 1:4 subject brightnesses, obtained by placement of shadow on Zone IV and developing to yield Zone VI or a slightly higher value for the sunlit skin. When less vigorous effects are desired, raise the shadow placement to Zone V, and give the negative normal-minus development. (Refer to page 94 for shadow control in synchro-sunlight.)

Occasionally, strong top light can be employed, but the thing to guard against always is the forlorn effect of a highlighted nose in a face of otherwise crepuscular gloom. This is usually the result of taking an "average reading" of subject, sky, and other elements within the field of the meter, so that the indicated placement is too high and the shadowed parts of the face fall too low on the scale. In such high-contrast subjects, with most of the face in shadow, it is advisable to place

36a. Edward Weston. Made with a Hasselblad camera, with no fill-in light.

36b. Michael Macauley. Made with a Hasselblad camera, in full shade.

the shadow values on Zone V and give a greatly reduced development, or else employ the water-bath technique or the two-solution development (see page 78).

The illusion of light is a relative matter. When most of the subject is in shadow, the shadow values have greater emotional impact than when sunlit areas are predominant; such shadowed subjects can be rendered lighter in tone than usual. It is perfectly possible to photograph in sharp noon sunlight, provided the dominant shadow values are carefully controlled. For an example, see Figure 15.

If sunlight portraits are made in an environment of low brightness, shadow values are astonishingly low, usually far lower than is apparent to the eye. This is especially true if the reflected light is dominantly greenish, since the eye responds to this color more than does the panchromatic film. Misjudgment of photographic brightness in such a case is common. To avoid black shadows, either fill in with appropriate supplemental light, or use special control of exposure and development (see Book 2, pp. 95-110).

A very satisfactory use of sunlight is in conjunction with open skylight with a well-shielded lens directed into the sun; that is, with the sun at a sufficient angle behind the subject to avoid unpleasant points of light on nose or cheek. It is advisable then to place the shadow values on Zone V or in certain cases where smoothness is desired, on Zone VI. The sunlit areas, being minute and of obviously great brilliancy, may go very white (Zone VIII or IX) in the final print. (However, should some texture in these sunlit areas be required, water-bath or two-solution development will help.) Reflectors are not desirable in such cases, because if the reflected light illuminates the entire face from below or from one side, its artificiality is apparent. If any reflector is used, it should be above the camera, thereby giving the effect of light coming down from the sky.

Unfavorable effects may result from glare reflected from the ground, light clothing, or other light surfaces. The eye accepts natural-lighting effects that are accounted for by environment. The aspect of a person's face broadly illuminated from ground glare usually is acceptable if the source of this illumination is part of the general scene. But in a photograph of a head that does not include the environment, this ground-glare effect may be ambiguous, and therefore disturbing. Watch out for this at beaches, on snow fields, on bright pavements, and in like places.

Portraits taken in sunlight on snow have a rather short range of values because of the strong environmental reflection. While the allover intensity is high, the relationship between shadows and highlights is usually gratifyingly balanced. Unfortunately, the reflected light may be dominantly from *below*, and care may be necessary to avoid unnatural effects, which appear unnatural chiefly when the source of illumination is not included in the picture area.

Sunlight at a sharp angle is much more manageable if the subject is photographed in profile rather than in a full-face position. Remember that it is difficult to get a valid meter reading on small areas, such as a part of the face, unless special equipment is used. For this information, see Book 1 (p. 64) on tube attachment for the Weston Master Exposure Meter, and Book 2 (p. 63) on the S.E.I. Exposure Photometer. A satisfactory method is to use a gray card of about the same reflective intensity as the skin (and of sufficient area to fill the field of the meter), and to take a meter reading on the card held in the sunlight. Its over-all value should closely approximate flat, unhighlighted but fully sunlit

Environmental Portraiture

The foregoing relates chiefly to portraiture of figure, or of head alone, without consideration for significant environment. A very important branch of portraiture can be called "environmental," because it includes a logical or a symbolic environment that intensifies or interprets the mood of the subject itself. I am not referring to literal environments—businessman in his office, doctor in his surgical smock—but to expressive environments. For example, a prominent and strong-willed public official might be photographed in an environment of rocks, or steel girders, to convey the mood of strength and endurance. The portrait of the young woman in Figure 38 is an example of this approach; her environment suggests her character. I hesitate to give further examples, as I do not wish the reader to be unduly influenced by my ideas; in this phase of photography the photographer's personal interpretations and reactions are paramount and should not be influenced by the concepts of other photographers. I urge all serious photographers to think along these expressive lines, and to avoid whenever possible the merely literal interpretations and associations.

39. Portrait (by Cedric Wright). Made under covered porch, natural skylight; background at angle to pick up light from left-hand porch opening. Figure itself near to right-hand opening. An excellent example of direct, honest portraiture. A large Graflex camera was used.

Photography in sunlight often involves a serious problem of extreme values that can be solved only by the addition of light—either flash, tungsten, or reflected light. The casual phrase "throwing a little light into the shadow" has a familiar sound, and is responsible for many esthetic failures. In the first place, no matter how extreme the contrast of light and shade may be, the photographer must first become aware of the *quality* of light in both the illuminated and the shadowed parts of the image. The mood of the light is of far greater significance than its mere photometric value, and that mood must be preserved. A head in sunlight, for instance, may give the impression of brilliant, enveloping light and yet the shadowed areas may actually have such low value as to lie beyond the range of adequate photographic treatment. In outdoor portraits it is difficult to control in the negative with any semblance of appropriate mood a brightness range of more than 1:16. This relates to a zonal placement of Zones III to VII inclusive; shadows lower than Zone III lose body and texture, high values above Zone VII may be "blocked." Compensation for greater range can only result in some "flattening" of the high values, or in some "deadening" of the shadows.

Units of Exposure

At this point we should introduce the "units-of-exposure" idea as an aid to visualization of the final print and to the balancing of subject-brightness values. In the section on Synchro-sunlight (page 94) some detailed applications will be demonstrated with flash. When flash is used, the computations are based on the known intensity of the flashlamp, but with reflectors (and steady-burning lights) their effect is measurable directly by an exposure meter (see Book 2, p. 49).

In the chart below the third line from the top represents what I term Exposure Units—with 1 unit opposite Zone 1. As the zones progress geometrically, so do the exposure units; the relative units of exposure are clearly shown for any zone, for relative lens stops, and for the Weston scale. A practical application of the units-of-exposure idea would be:

You visualize a portrait head in the print as having a Zone IV to VI placement of shadow and sunlit skin values (a range of 1:4). Assume that the *actual* brightness of the subject is 25 to 400 (a range of 1:16). If you place the sunlit skin on Zone VI, the shadows fall on Zone II (which represent 2 units of exposure). To raise these values to Zone IV (8 units of exposure), you must add 6 units; as the 6 units are also added to the sunlit areas of the head, the actual brightness range will be 8:38, or a little over 1:4. With reflectors you add light to the shadow areas until your meter shows a Zone IV value (or any desired value); with flash, as I have said, you must compute the values.

Rel. Lens Stop F/	64	45	32	22	16	11	8	5.6	4	2.8
Rel. Exp. for V	1/32	1/16	1/8	1/4	1/2	1	2	4	8	16
Rel. Exp. For I	1/2	1	2	4	8	16	32	64	128	256
Weston Scale	—	U	—	—	A	↓	C	—	O	—
ZONES	O	I	II	III	IV	V	VI	VII	VIII	IX

40. Alfred Stieglitz in His Gallery. Made with a Zeiss Contax, 50mm lens. A cross light from two windows; no supplementary light. Walls of gallery were very light and provided ample illumination for the shadowed areas of the face. The miniature camera makes possible unlimited opportunities for serious, revealing portraiture.

The quality and direction of the shadows as they naturally occur determines the quality and the direction of the reflected light to be employed. An unnatural effect will result if the reflected light is of different quality and direction from the natural shadow light. In Figure 41a you see a head photographed in sunlight, but with the immediate environment of rather dark wood producing a low shadow value. The sunlit portions of the skin were placed on Zone VI, and the important shadows fell on Zone II. This range of 1:16 is very harsh.

You can visualize the desired value of the shadows as on about Zone IV, yet if you so place them, the sunlit portions are raised to Zone VIII, and a general flatness, which destroys brilliance and clarity, may obtain Figure 41b. You can, however, as in Figure 41c, illuminate the shadows from a diffuse source and from the same general direction as the existing weak reflected light. The quality of this introduced light remains about the same as that of the original shadow light. You have increased the illumination in the shadow areas without altering its character. In this case you have added about 2 units of exposure (see tables on pages 95 and 96), which places the shadow values approximately on Zone III, but has not appreciably affected the higher values. In Figure 41d you have also added 8 units of light, but this time you have used a "sharper" source, and applied it from a different direction. You immediately see that diffuse highlights appear at different shadowed areas of the face than in Figure 41c, and you also note false secondary shadows that do not relate to the facial structure as revealed by the main source of light—the sun.

When reflecting sunlight into small areas, the broader the source of illumination and the softer the reflecting material (that is, the more diffuse), the more "naturalistic" the result will be. The great differences between light reflected from a diffuse reflective surface such as a sheet of white cloth, a surface of crinkled tin or aluminum foil, and a plain mirror, are apparent to all who have used these devices. It is impossible to describe and illustrate all the dismal effects of the faulty use of reflectors (and artificial "boosting" light), but these basic examples should stimulate the photographer to recognize others of inadequate application.

Of course, the foregoing should not suggest that special unrealistic effects are not valid. As in all phases of the general approach of these books, I first concentrate on a naturalistic point of departure, then suggest and encourage creative deviations. Quite often in nature a photograph shows some apparently unrealistic effect—such as a strong reflection from snow—that would become "realistic" if the source of the environmental reflection appeared in the photograph. Comprehension of any photographic image is based on both factually stated elements of the scene and implied elements and conditions.

In the vast and swiftly growing literature on photography I find much emphasis on expensive formulas, tricks, and rigid esthetic "principles." Most of these formulas are invalid because they do not permit the individual to explore his own world of vision and concept. As I continue to write, teach, and photograph I am increasingly aware of the futility of expressive formulas, and of the importance of a competent technique. I sincerely hope that my technical recommendations in these Basic Photo books will not be misinterpreted as anything but concepts to clarify the problems of individual expression.

41a.

41b.

41c.

41d.

41a-d. Examples of fill-in light quality. 41a represents harsh subject-brightness range (Zones II-VI), exposed and developed normally (placement of skin values on Zone VI). 41b represents effect of placing shadow values on Zone IV (normal exposure and development); the high values of the sunlit skin fall on Zone VIII and are "blocked." 41c shows the effect of adding 2 units of illumination to the shadows; the shadow values are on Zone III. 41d shows the effect of adding about 8 units of illumination from a sharply directed source—note the obvious shadows on background and face as well as the secondary highlights on the face.

Unfortunately the reproduction process does not convey tonal subtleties; the reader is urged to make many experiments along these lines and find out for himself the many problems of interpretation involved in the use of fill-in illumination.

SYNCHRO-SUNLIGHT

In synchro-sunlight photography the shadows are illuminated from an artificial light source (flashlamp). This subject is treated extensively in Book 5, but it is advisable here to study the simpler aspects of application, which are more difficult than the average photographer realizes. It is my experience that the usual synchro-flash rules as given on manufacturers' instruction sheets often lead to unsatisfactory technical and esthetic results—usually gross overillumination of the shadows and an entirely false illusion of light. You cannot obtain a realistic and natural effect from this combination of lights unless you keep natural causes in mind, and avoid illogical arrangements.

Two dominant problems arise: the direction of the light, and the intensity of illumination. A portrait out of doors, for example, illuminated by sunlight and diffuse skylight, shows—irrespective of the brightness of the shadow areas—a logical direction of light. It is a broad, even light, with a suggestion of coming from above. Now if you illuminate the shadowed area of a face by a sharp, bright flash from, say, off to one side of the camera, you see rather sharp secondary highlights and sharp-edged shadows falling within the natural shadow. The illusion of diffuse skylight is lost. To be logical, you must have the supplementary light come from the general direction of skylight, and it should be diffuse. It may also be necessary, if a large part of the face is in shadow and the diffuse skylight comes largely from above, to add a small amount of supplemental light from very near the axis of the lens—merely to balance inequalities of illumination on the face.

42. Test to Establish Guide Number. Such tests should be made outdoors at night, distant from any reflecting surface. The flash factors will then be at minimum value, and when photographs are made in reflective environment, compensation should be made. A large neutral card of about 35% reflectivity (about the same as Caucasian skin) is held at an angle of about 30 to 45° off the perpendicular to the direction of the flash (to avoid direct glare). A head should be placed before it to serve as a check on the general all-over values. If the head is appreciably nearer the flash than the card, it will of course be rendered as higher opacity in the negative. Then proceed with the test described on page 97.

The volume of light applied must be carefully chosen if the effect is to be natural. To determine the amount, first determine the desired zonal placement of the shadow values. Assume that you have placed the sunlit values of the face (the flat of the cheek at about 45° to the sun) on Zone VI. Your visualization calls for shadows on about Zone IV. But they actually fall on Zone II. The supplemental light should be only enough to raise shadow values to the desired Zone IV. Here is the disposition of the values:

PLACEMENT OF VALUES 1

Zones	I	II	III	IV	V	VI
Exposure units	(1)	(2)	(4)	(8)	(16)	(32)
Meter reading (in c.p.sq.ft.)		25				400
Brightness range		(1)				(16)
Our shadow values fall on		X				
We desire them to fall on				X		
We add 8 units of exposure*		(8)				(8)
The effective units of exposure then are				(10)		(40)
And the approximate placement				X		X
And the approximate brightness range				(1)		(4)

Note that the sunlit areas also pick up the supplementary or reflected light, but that the effective exposure difference is small. If you use the appropriate quality of light—and at proper direction to the subject—the results should be quite "naturalistic."

Now suppose you have the same disposition of the original values.

PLACEMENT OF VALUES 2

Zones	I	II	III	IV	V	VI	VII	Brightness Range
Exposure units	(1)	(2)	(4)	(8)	(16)	(32)		1:32
Meter reading (in c.p.sq.ft.)		25				400		1:16
We add a volume of flash		(32)				(32)		
The effective exposure units are (placements, Zones VI+ and VII)						(40)	(64)	about 1 to 1½

This close range of brightnesses would be unnatural and unpleasant.

You have considered the general shadow value of the face as of Zone II value (2 units). Assume that the values of certain parts of the face such as eye sockets are lower—say of Zone I value (1 unit). A fill-in light *at the lens axis* will "boost" such areas in illumination and will also provide a "catchlight" in the eyes.

---

*With flash it is simpler to add light in geometric units of 2, 4, 8, 16, etc., while with reflected or steady-burning light we can apply any number of exposure units (any volume of light), as the effect is directly measurable with an exposure meter.

With a fill-in light at the lens (giving 1 unit of illumination, to the 1 unit of dark shadow on the face as mentioned above):

PLACEMENT OF VALUES 3

Zones	I	II	III	IV	V	VI	Brightness Range
Exposure units	(1)	(2)	(4)	(8)	(16)	(32)	1:32
Meter readings (in c.p.sq.ft.)	13	25				400	1:32
Relative units of exposure of above	(1)	(2)				(32)	
We add 1 unit of axis illumination	(1)	(1)				(1)	
We add 8 units of shadow illumination		(8)				(8)	
The effective (accumulated) exposure units are	(2)				(11)	(41)	
And the approximate placements are		X			X	X	About 1:20*

Note that the actual exposure need not be changed—the difference of 32 and 40 or 41 units for the sunlit values is not critical, although if precision is desired, the lens stop can be slightly reduced. But the brightness range of the subject is profoundly changed.

Guide numbers for flashlamps for any zonal placement can be computed with ease once the basic factor is established. The procedure for making this test is as follows: Set up the subject out of doors at night, or in a very large dark room—to avoid environmental reflections, and select any standard flashlamp. Insert it in a diffusion reflector (a brushed aluminum surface is excellent, or an ordinary reflector with a diffusing screen). The subject can be the head or figure of a person, or a card of about 35% reflectivity. (Fig. 42).

Make a series of exposures at a given stop (noting the proper exposure index of the film used), placing the flash at varying distances from the subject. Base the first exposure on the published guide numbers for the particular lamp used. The number is based on the distance-to-subject x the stop number. Dividing the stop number into the guide number gives the proper distance at which to place the flash; dividing the distance into the guide number gives the proper stop number to use. NOTE: as the stops are in geometrical progression, doubling the guide number represents *four* times the effective light. To double the exposure value, multiply the guide number by the square root of 2—roughly, 1.4.

This first exposure, based on the manufacturer's guide number, will probably be less than required. Follow with exposures of increasing value, either moving the flash closer to the subject, or using a larger stop. Suggested exposures might be as listed below. Assuming you are using a flashlamp of guide number 160 (for the film used, and at "open" or 1/25-second exposure) your first exposure would be at f/16 with the flash 10 feet from the subject. Then proceed with a series of exposures, as follows:

---

*The brightness range of main shadow to sunlit value is about 1:4, but small pockets of shadow not reached by the principal shadow illumination are rendered effectively on Zone II.

f/16	Distance	8 ft.		128
		7 ft.		112
	Distance	6 ft.		96
		5 ft.	Effective guide number	80
f/11	Distance	6 ft.		66
		5 ft.		55
f/8	Distance	6 ft.		48

Develop the negatives for "normal" Zone VI values (as determined by the basic tests outlined in Book II) and select that one which most closely approximates the normal Zone VI value. This will suggest the approximate guide number to be used to achieve the desired opacity value, in a normally developed negative, for a Zone VI brightness value (such as average skin in sunlight—35% reflectivity). Remember, different film, reflectors, reflective environments, and different shutter speeds will all modify the value of the flash factor!

Now that you have the desired guide number for Zone VI placement, it is a simple matter to determine the numbers required for placing skin values on any zone. The following table is based on an arbitrary factor of 96 for Zone VI placement of skin values:

Zones	I	II	III	IV	V	VI	VII	VIII	IX
Exposure units	1	2	4	8	16	32	64	128	256
Effective guide numbers	536	384	268	192	134	**96**	77	48	37.5
Effective guide numbers (round numbers)	560	400	280	200	140	**100**	70	50	35

Rounding off the numbers will simplify calculations.

An example of the use of the above table: If you wish to add 8 units of exposure, you find you should use a guide number of 200. If the basic exposure for sunlit skin for Zone VI placement is 1/25 second at f/22, the flash should be placed at about 9 feet from the subject (22/200=9).

Once you have determined the guide number for a given flashlamp and a given film, you can by simple interpolation determine the numbers for other flashlamps by comparing their effective published guide numbers with the published number of the first flashlamp. For example:

Published guide number for lamp used	180
Effective guide number for lamp used	100
Published guide number for other lamp	220
Effective factor for other lamp	120 (approximately)

Formula: 180 : 100 :: 220 : X

Similar computations will adjust the guide numbers for different film speeds. The relative value of light emitted from different reflectors can be determined by inserting tungsten lamps of equal power in the reflectors and measuring the light from them directed on a white card. Lamp-to-card distance must be the same throughout.

I strongly suggest that you execute the test outlined above carefully, and that you compile a table of flash factors for various lamps, film speeds, and reflectors for immediate reference. This will save you much work in the field Remember, once the basic factor is established for *any* flash lamp in reference to a desired exposure value, the factors for all lamps, various film speeds, and various reflectors, can be determined by simple calculations.

The value of diffusing screens, "bounced light," etc. must not be overlooked. Frequently the raw flash from the flashgun or extension reflector is of harsh quality—especially noticeable when a duplication of skylight quality is desired. This light can be softened by using diffusing screens over the flashlamp; ordinary handkerchiefs can be used if necessary. The absorption factor of the diffusing material can be determined by putting an ordinary tungsten lamp in the reflector and noting the decrease of light with the diffusing material used. Additions to the table on Page 97 would include the effective factors of the lamps with various diffusing devices applied.

"Bounced light" is merely light from flashlamp or other illuminant that has been directed to a reflective surface (of diffusing quality) and then to the subject. The larger this reflecting surface, the "softer" the reflected light. A large piece of white cardboard or a sheet on a rigid frame will serve admirably. The effective value of the "bounced light" can be determined by making photometric measurements at night with a tungsten lamp as the light source, or, of course, measuring the increment by densotometric readings on flashlamp-exposed negatives. The inverse-square law applies equally to light from flashlamp or illuminated surface; but the distance from lamp to surface may vary without practical effect if *all* of the light from the flashlamp is reflected from the surface.

In making tests with various lamp reflectors we must not overlook the fact that many reflectors have a "focal length"; that is, their curvatures "direct" the beam and the inverse square law does not hold (from the actual position of the lamp) as it would with a lamp "in the open" without reflector. To check this point, take any standard reflector, place an ordinary tungsten lamp in it and direct the lamp towards a white wall or card at, say, 3 feet from the center of the lamp. Take the meter reading from the wall. Then, move the lamp and reflector back to 6 feet; take the meter reading and compare. If the reflector has no "focal length" the reading should be $\frac{1}{4}$ that of the 3-foot position. Try again at 12 feet—the reading should be $\frac{1}{16}$ that at the 3-foot position. However, if the reflector had a focal-length of 2 feet— that is, its focal point would be 2 feet *behind* the lamp— the effective distance of the above positions would be 5 ft., 8 ft., and 14 ft.—or an effective exposure *ratio* of 1, 6.4, and 20. A ratio of 1, 4, 9, and 16 can be established by placing the *lamp* at a distance of 3, 8, and 18 feet from the wall. $(3 + 2 = 5; \ 8 + 2 = 10; \ 13 + 2 = 15; \ 18 + 2 = 20)$

In Book 5 of this series this discussion is amplified, and the problem of variation in flash factors due to environments of various reflectivities, such as an interior with white walls, will be discussed. But with flash used out of doors with sunlight or bright daylight it is assumed that environmental reflections are at a minimum.

43. Church, Cape Cod. A subject of rather extreme brightness range, intentionally rendered in high contrast to accentuate the mood of glaring whites and clear dark sky. The gilded rooster atop the steeple is glittering in the sun and is absolutely white in the print. The whites of the structure lie between Zones VIII and IX. The open door is absolutely black and falls on Zone O value in the print. Exposure was reduced, development was normal plus. A Zeiss G-4 filter (similar to a Wratten G) was used.

ARCHITECTURE AND INDUSTRY

No field of professional photography is more exacting than architecture. We speak casually of "architectural photography," when the phrase "photography of architecture" is much more apt. "Architectural photography" indicates a certain kind of approach to general work in which intellectual and emotional factors are organized in a formal way. Except when architectural subjects are used as pictorial material, the photography of architecture has a specific function—to interpret and present the work of the architect. Ethics are involved on both sides. The architect should not influence the photographer to distort or exaggerate, and the photographer should acquire an intimate understanding of the problem before him.

The necessity for "writing the program" is apparent to anyone who attempts work of this type. In Book 6 of this series programs are developed for individual photographs that have a specific practical function. In brief, the procedure in undertaking photography of architecture would be:

1. Consultation with the architect on the purpose and use of the photographs.

2. Study of the architecture with reference to its function, its style, its composition; relation to its environment; structure and materials used.

3. Establishment of a consistent interpretation: determining the most effective general contrast scale, "mood" of the print, print color, size, and presentation of the print.

All these factors should be listed and thought about before any photograph is made. In addition, before the camera is even set up you should make a thorough survey of the subject to observe the effects of various lighting conditions. While this may sound complex to those who merely pick up a camera, go to a place, make some exposures, and think that is all there is to it, I assure them from direct experience that a little time spent in thinking and planning will guarantee superior results.

Architectural Exteriors

To couple an appropriate interpretation of form and substance with the most revealing point of view presents problems of considerable difficulty. While many liberties can be taken with the rendition of natural objects, photography of architecture usually requires a certain realism and accuracy. To this end, the camera should be level with the subject, and it is imperative that the back of the camera—that is, the plane of the negative—be parallel to the plane of the object, both horizontally and vertically, in order to avoid distortion. Just as a rising front on the camera is essential to preserve vertical accuracies of form, so is the falling front essential in most views looking *down*—for example, upon buildings or gardens. If a down view is from a considerable height, convergence can be used to great advantage, but such convergence, I repeat, must be definite and precise and never indicate a careless distortion. Any deviation from rectilinear presentation should be made apparent, leaving no doubt in the spectator's mind that a conscious deviation exists and that it serves an intentional purpose. A slight convergence of lines merely indicates carelessness, and the purposeless "angle shot" can be a most false and disturbing approach.

It is difficult, if not impossible, to photograph structures independent of their environments. As a rule the structure and its environment constitute a unit of design. A well-designed building takes full advantage of its situation, and is related in some way to its surrounding terrain. It should be the purpose of the photograph to suggest this function and this design as well as to give a clear image of the physical reality. If a building is illuminated by sunlight, the illusion of sunlight should be preserved in the photograph; it is a rather cheap trick to overemphasize shadows and exaggerate "pattern effects." In the magnificent early photographs (circa 1850) of cathedrals by Le Secq and Roger Fenton, devotion to the object itself was always evident, and in spite of exceedingly crude equipment and materials, the illusion of substance and of formal relationships was handsomely conveyed.

After reaching an understanding of the structure in relation to its environment, you will, of course, stress or minimize the environment, as required. As I have already suggested, a building in a city may require a very tight composition that practically fills the picture area, simply to avoid conflict with the adjacent buildings. A structure designed to take advantage of light and space in a wide, open setting would benefit through composition in large space. I advise the reader to examine architectural books and periodicals, by no means overlooking early European and American volumes containing steel engravings and other graphic presentations. This will give a background of appreciation for significant point of view and awareness of scale and form.

One of the drawbacks of much present-day photography of architecture is an inherent sentimentality of viewpoint. Many such photographs are made from a point of view that results in a composition having little to do with the design and the orientation of the structure. However, certain stylized viewpoints may be very useful. See Figure 45, for which the camera was set squarely opposite the house and there is little effect of volume or perspective. The image is merely a façade, closely approaching the precision of a formal architectural drawing. In any series of photographs of one architectural subject the inclusion of a few of this severe-façade type may strengthen the general impression of reality.

Again, the rendering of a building in fairly small scale against a large landscape, or against an open expanse of sky, accentuates the environmental impression. Another extreme, and one that is very useful, is the judicious employment of short-focus lenses in order to include "interrupting forms" of near-by objects, such as a gate or foliage, in sharp focus, all of which tends to suggest special dimensions and to exaggerate scale. But mere exaggeration of scale, without retaining a proper relationship between elements of the subject, can create interpretative havoc.

Unfortunately, the indiscriminate use of wide-angle lenses is a common misapplication in photography of architecture. Especially unpleasant in architectural interiors, it also creates a very false impression of exterior scale, and of the structure in relation to its environment. When (owing to physical conditions) it becomes necessary to use a wide-angle lens, a more or less complete stylization is indicated. In other words, it is better to produce a greatly exaggerated wide-angle effect that will be appreciated as such than a moderate exaggeration that may only perplex the spectator.

The question of scale has always plagued photographers. True scale can be expressed only by direct comparison. Emotional scale is quite another thing, and can be suggested by the proper use of interrupting forms, as suggested above.

101

44. In South Carolina Town. In the original print there is detail in the darkest parts of the image. The camera is precisely orientated; it was placed a little off center (to the right) to include the distant steeple, but the camera back was parallel to the façade of the house.

Perspective and other associated impressions derived in this way augment the feeling of space and distance in the print, and this approach is valid, and far more exciting than organization in the middle and the far distance alone. Further, the spectator's orientation is of such great importance that the illusion of scale must be either quite accurate or exceedingly stylized.

In most architecture we recognize certain elements as basic "keys" of scale; steps, ordinary windows, and bricks are, with few exceptions, within consistent limits of size. Furthermore, as structures are inhabited and designed for use, it would seem important to include life and activity, if for no other reason than to suggest function and scale.

In work of this type always take meter readings from a direction approximating that of the lens axis. Many structural surfaces are highly reflective, so that even a slight difference of angle changes the meter readings. It is also good, when composing an architectural photograph, to examine the subject through a monochromatic viewing filter. The disposition of shadows and color values in the subject is then more clearly perceived, and the translation of color into appropriate grays is more easily visualized. A building of a definite color surrounded by green foliage or by structures of contrasting color can be brilliant

102

to the eye but drab in a photograph. It is necessary, where colors are involved, to establish arbitrary but appropriate tonal values and contrasts through the proper use of filters.

The tonal relationship of the structure to sky and foliage, especially, is an ever present problem. Since architectural subjects are chiefly photographed for reproduction, in which case very close tone gradations will suffer, it is a good rule to control all important separations by at least one zone of the scale; separation between structure and sky may be about two zones. The usual gray or middle-toned colored roofing and wall materials are very difficult to separate from the sky, yet if an overstrong filter is used, the shadows may be rendered so deep that effective detail is lost. At such times the use of a blue filter can be very helpful, for at least it will render the sky light, although foliage may then be photographed too dark. Obviously, when the structure is in both sun and shade the image will be of rather full scale, and control of shadows is then of extreme importance. If you work for the sunlit areas alone, shadows and sky may suffer, and if you work for the shadows alone, high values and sky may suffer. Compromise is inevitable. See Figure 44 for an example.

In spite of the necessity for revealing substance accurately throughout the subject, certain minor parts of the image can be rendered completely black, thus serving as an excellent basic key for the general tonality. Unless near views of windows require some rendition of interior details, the openings of windows and doors can be rendered as black. Pure whites seldom exist in architecture, although highlights appearing on glass or polished metal should be rendered as pure white in the print. Even the whitest plaster or paint suggest substance, and very subtle treatment of the high tones is required to preserve the illusion of surface and brilliancy. A white stucco building, for example, may have one wall in shadow and the other in very bright sunlight. This effect may be accentuated by using a G filter and less-than-normal exposure to render the sky rather dark, and by photographing from an angle that shows most of the building in shadow. Consult current architectural magazines for pictorial suggestions on the lighting of exteriors, and after a short time you will, it is hoped, recognize the falsities that are frequently introduced for spectacular effect without regard for integrity of interpretation of the structure or the materials composing it.

Selection of the most revealing angle of light is also important. That direction should be used which best reveals surface textures without distorting structural form. For example, a very acute light might accentuate the textures of a brick wall but at the same time cast perplexing shadows under windows and copings.

A pattern that is obvious to the eye may, when reduced to the confines of the print, fall below the limits of convincing visual resolution. In the interpretation of a brick building, the images of the individual bricks must be resolved in the picture or the sense of substance will be lacking. Hence some key, such as a near corner or extension of wall, should be included to support the conviction of the material used. In a series of photographs of one structure details of materials can be presented separately that will "explain" the more inclusive images.

The photographer is always confronted with the necessity of showing subtle variations that will differentiate such surfaces as those of plaster, smooth concrete, and simple painted wood. Yet it is sometimes extremely difficult to photograph an intricately textured building under ordinary sunlight conditions because of the great range of brightnesses between sunlit and shadowed areas. One solution to this problem is the use of multiple exposure, as follows:

Before the sun strikes the side of the building being photographed, give an exposure that will place the entire structure on Zone IV or V of the exposure scale. Then, without in any way disturbing or jarring the camera, wait until the angular shafts of sunlight fall on the building and then give a second exposure, calculating it so that the sunlit areas will be effectively placed between two and three zones above their placement when in full shade. Remember that all values are *accumulative*—but on a logarithmic ratio. Hence, shadow plus shadow shows a greater actual effect than does shadow plus sunlight. The following chart will help describe this effect:

Zones	1	II	III	IV	V	VI	VII	Brightness Range
Exposure units	1	2	4	8	16	32	64	
Shadow exposure (entire building) (c/ft²)			50			(50)		
Sunlight exp. (sunlit areas) (c/ft²)			50			400		1 to 8
(shadow areas get additional exp.)			(50)					
Accumulated exp. values (c/ft²)				100		450		1 to 4½
Expressed in Exposure Units				8		36		1 to 4½
If shadow values were placed on II								
Shadow exposure (entire building)		50				(50)		
Sunlight exposure (sunlit areas) (c/ft²)			50			400		1 to 8
Accumulated exposure units		2+4=6				32+2=34		
Accumulated exposure values (c/ft²)			75			425		1 to 5.6

In the second case, the all-over shadow values were placed on Zone II, yielding 2 units of exposure. The sunlit areas, placed on VI, would give a Zone III placement of the shadows. Hence, the accumulated value for the shadowed areas is II plus III, or 6 exposure units, and the accumulated value for the sunlit areas is II plus VI, or 34 exposure units. It is obvious that a considerable control is possible by this multiple-exposure process, but neither subject nor camera can be allowed to move the slightest degree during and between the various exposures.

It is frequently necessary to interpret details of structure and design not only for their own qualities, but to support and explain qualities of the subject that cannot be revealed in large, inclusive images. Here again you need emphasis on substance, light, space, and scale, and consistent clarity throughout the image is essential. It may not be easy to suggest scale without the inclusion of a recognizable object, and I believe it is entirely possible to include hands, tools, or even a small rule, without distracting from the realistic aspect of the object. Typical examples of architectural detail include hardware, lighting fixtures, details of construction, close interpretations of various materials, and ornamental designs.

Architectural Interiors

Before the advent of practical artificial light, interiors were photographed entirely with light from windows or skylights, which of course imposed strict limitations. While perfectly satisfactory images can be made with very low intensities of light when the reciprocity effect (see Book 2, pp. 13, 59) is taken into consideration, the almost insurmountable problems of extreme contrast and flare arise when the source of light, such as window or doorway, is included within the picture. Many ingenious methods have been devised to overcome such effects, such as hanging a dark cloth outside the window within the field of view, exposing the interior fully (assume there is another source of illumination!) and then removing this cloth for a second exposure on the same film that will record the exterior scene; the use of highly dilute developers, such as pyrocatechin and other compensators (Book 2, pp. 107-08); or the subsequent manipulation and local reduction of the "burnt-up" portions of the negative; but no entirely satisfactory solution has ever been achieved. The photography of interiors, at least by present-day standards, demands some use of artificial light.

Certain interior details, however, can be made with natural light from windows, with or without the use of reflectors, and a realistic feeling will result in most cases. Remember that the light values may be exceedingly low and areas in shadow may reflect practically no light of any photographic consequence. Under such conditions it is safe to assume that exposure can be very full, and unless the light source appears within the field of view, development can be carried quite far. The reciprocity effect makes it almost impossible to overexpose extremely low brightness values seriously. A typical example may be an interior fireplace illuminated from several distant windows, in all comprising a very weak source of light. Except when interiors are illuminated with powerful crosslight and contain strong, massive shadows, development of the negative can be quite full, since the brightness scale of such subjects is usually very short.

In the case of an interior where the window in the field of view looks out upon a garden, or on some exterior that must be accurately interpreted, the solution of the problem can be that mentioned above, as follows: Attach an opaque black cloth snugly outside the window frame. Photograph the interior of the room with the existing natural light (or if none is available, with artificial light). Then, at the time of day at which the external scene is most attractive, remove the cloth and, without moving or jarring the camera, expose for the external scene, placing its average values two zones *above* the placement of the values of the walls of the interior in the first exposure. If the exposures are calculated correctly, development should be normal. With this procedure, the realistic relationship of interior and exterior values will be preserved. If interior and exterior values are similar, the exterior view will suggest a photomural within the room! With color film, it is imperative that the lighting be consistent in character; that is, if floodlamps or flashlamps are used to balance interior and exterior lighting, they must be of the blue "daylight" quality.

I caution the student experimenting with these devices to observe and work for consistent lighting effects. In other words, if a shaft of sunlight comes through one window on the right and falls across the floor, but lighting of the subsequently exposed scene outside any other window is in a different direction, a false effect will certainly result.

The illusion of substance and light should be preserved with special care in the high textured areas of the subject. It is now generally agreed that detail and textures can be forfeited in the dark, shadowed areas of the subject with less unpleasant effect than if lost in the high textured areas. However, large areas of low brightness must show adequate textural quality throughout.

Industrial Architecture

In the photography of industrial architecture, the interpretation of substance and scale is of even greater importance than in ordinary architectural work. The function of an industrial structure must be clearly understood. Pipes, conveyors, cable lines, and other elements must be seen and composed in relation to their function. Although there is a tendency to rely entirely on the spectacular aspects of industrial architecture, the engineer demands more than dramatic images. The inclusion of unrelated objects makes it all the more difficult to understand the function of the structure portrayed, especially if it is already complex.

In many industrial environments extreme haze and smoke seriously affect the quality of light, as has already been noted, and the photographer must resort to careful use of filters to preserve adequate contrast without distorting important values. One phase of industrial photography that is very difficult to manage is minimizing the apparent dirt and disorder of the industrial environment. In many cases this perfectly understandable confusion may have intriguing photographic possibilities. In fact, a junkyard is a veritable gold mine of forms and textures. But what may appear to the eye as a normal aspect of some great factory may well appear in the photograph as an unfortunate mass of dirt and disorder that will arouse the objections of the designer and the plant executive if presented in a print. To clean up this inevitable disorder just for the picture may be impossible, and at best would give an impression of improbable tidyness. It is better for the photographer to minimize aspects of confusion by careful selection of viewpoint and elimination of much immediate foreground detail. In many cases the cluttered detail of a foundry yard, for example, can be hidden by the use of some larger interrupting form, such as an orderly stack of pipes or a large casting. The client will appreciate the care the photographer exercises in this regard.

In many cases the interiors of large industrial plants are so vast as to make photography with artificial light impractical except with unusually extensive lighting equipment. Such interiors can be rendered by their normal illumination with very long exposures; but again, if light sources are included in the field of view, a compensating developer such as pyrocatechin (Book 2, p. 117) is indicated. Multiple exposures are likely to be impractical in a plant. There is no doubt that optically coated lens and modern antihalation negative material are of great value under these conditions.

As the brightnesses are very low, it may be difficult to get accurate readings by direct methods except with a sensitive exposure photometer such as the S.E.I. One indirect way is to use a white card. Take the reading from it and place it on Zone VIII of the scale. If the light is too weak even to read in this way with an ordinary meter, take the reading at the darkest point of the interior with an incident-light meter. Also, determining exposure for the white card near the light source and multiplying this value by the inverse-square factor, with proper consideration for reciprocity effect, gives excellent results. This is the procedure: **exposure-near-light-source x square of distance of subject from light source = correct exposure for white card at subject-distance from light source.** Placing the white-card brightness on Zone VIII assures placement of other brightnesses on related Zones. Conventional procedure involves taking the "exposure" from the white card and multiplying by 5. This represents placement of the white-card brightness (about 85% reflectivity) a little above Zone VII.

It is difficult to overexpose a subject of very low brightness. Also, as the contrast range, exclusive of the light source, is very short, some rather full development is indicated, though if light sources are included, either a protracted water bath or the use of a compensating formula is necessary. If exposures are very long, certain areas can be built up by the use of concealed flashlamps or with strong tungsten lights. (Refer to Book 5 for further details of interior illumination with artificial light.)

In photographing machinery, etc., with heavily shaded inner areas, a good balance of illumination can be achieved by the use of an electric torch. Direct its light with constant movement ("painting with light") over the shaded areas. Light can also be reflected onto deeply shaded areas by a mirror. All such applications of light will be spotty and uneven unless the sources are kept in constant motion and the areas are completely covered with equal amounts of illumination.

Industrial photography is frequently concerned with the photographic interpretation of the processes themselves. An interior assembly or a machine may have meaning only when shown in operation. This brings in a very complex problem of involved foreground and background relationships. If the photograph is merely that of the machine at close range, then the background should be minimized if not eliminated, but if the problem is an interpretation of a plant interior in which the machine is an integral part, there should be some logical relationship of value and scale between the machine and its environment. This may require extensive use of artificial light. However, daylight from skylights or windows, if it is adequate, always yields interesting and authentic effects. A certain amount of back lighting will augment the impression of depth.

Occasionally, the impression of machinery in motion can be achieved by making a time exposure of the machine in motion; then, with the machine stopped, complete the exposure. The static phase of the exposure should require about three-fourths the total exposure time.

The use of figures in industrial scenes presents a perplexing problem. Of course, in photographing actual processes of work the figure is logical and necessary. But in large general views of plant, mine, etc.,—or in stylized details of machinery, etc.,—the inclusion of a figure or figures (unless properly directed) will appear trite and disturbing. A figure included merely for "scale" can turn out to be a jarring note in an otherwise well-organized composition. The figure should always bear some dynamic and logical relationship to the whole.

Many industrial scenes are of vast expanse—great open-pit mines wherein men, shovels, and trains seem as mere toys; huge areas for settling, storage, etc., and complicated structures set in even more complicated environments. In most cases the colors may be drab and the layout (from the ground, at least) confusing. It is such subject matter that taxes the ingenuity of the photographer; he must literally create order out of chaos. He should carefully study the best industrial photography extant, referring to *Fortune Magazine* from its first issue, and to architectural and engineering publications. In sifting through a large body of material, the most powerful images will be obvious, and lessons will be learned in comparing the strong and revealing pictures with the commonplace and ineffectual ones. It is not the technique that is complicated in such pictures; the imaginative factors triumph. When studying a photograph, try to re-create the scene before the camera, and consider the procedures involved, especially the lens and camera adjustments required.

45. Copy (detail) "Saint Mary Magdalen," Pieter Coeck van Aelst (Flemish, 1502-1550), courtesy M. H. de Young Memorial Museum, San Francisco. Made with a Hasselblad camera in existing light in the museum.

OBJECTS OF ART

We have become so accustomed to seeing photographs of objects of art made in controlled artificial light that we have forgotten how beautiful the effects of sunlight or diffuse daylight can be for them. On page 110 I mention the copying of paintings and photographs in natural light; in working with jewelry, sculpture, and other three-dimensional objects, the same basic principles apply. However, background elements that do not perplex the photographer in copying paintings or other flat images can be very difficult to manage when working with objects in the round. Occasionally objects such as altar pieces or garden sculpture may be photographed in a related environment, but as a rule environmental effects only distract attention from the subject.

When working indoors with light from skylight or window it is a rather simple matter to control the intensity of a background screen by placing it at the required distance from the light source. Such a screen should be white on one side and rather dark gray on the other. Using one side or the other, a wide range of intensities can be attained. The screen should be large enough, of course, to fill the angle of view of the lens at all working distances. First, place the object to be photographed in the most favorable light, with shadows supported by diffuse reflections, if necessary, and then adjust the background so that the proper separation of values is achieved. The background brightness should be separated from both high and low values in the object by *at least* one zone. Use of a monochromatic viewing filter is very helpful in determining these relationships. Merely throwing enough light on an object to reveal its detail is by no means sufficient. Sculpture, for example, is usually executed in illumination of one general direction, or it may be designed for a certain directional lighting. It is important to study the sculpture in order to determine what this ideal direction of light is.

Frequently the tendency is to "dramatize," but the appropriate direction and intensity of light are of far greater importance than some merely striking arrangement of light and shade. A rich, enveloping, and revealing light is far more exciting in the end than a superficial theatrical effect. Any light from window or skylights is directional in character, but illumination from diffuse skylight out of doors is far more enveloping. Sunlight, too, can be extremely effective, and it is not difficult to control shadow-highlight relationships through proper use of diffuse reflectors, correct exposure placement, and related development. Background problems in outdoor light (diffuse or sunlight) are more difficult to master than those indoors. As variations in tone cannot be effected by changing the distance of the background, it is necessary to use a background screen of a desired tonality, or to shield it in some way from the light from the sky. In sunlight the values of any smooth surface can be changed somewhat by altering the angle of this surface to the sun, and thereby altering the reflection, but the variations of tone by this method are necessarily limited.

The surface upon which objects rest must also be considered. Sculpture that stands on a relatively small pedestal and is usually seen from a low viewpoint is not difficult to manage; the pedestal may show only as a small narrow strip at the base of the picture. But in photographing objects that are designed to be held in the hand or set upon flat surfaces, the direction of view is naturally down, and the surface upon which the object rests becomes, at least in part, its background. In this case materials must be selected with great care, and the joining of supporting surface and background must be worked out so that there are no distractions. A flat object can be suspended on a wall or an inclined plane as well as being laid flat on a horizontal surface. Even in diffuse light such an object casts a small shadow; this shadow may help or hinder the impression of edge and depth. Conventional museum technique favors the use of white backgrounds, commonly achieved by "opaquing" the negative. This is a very crude and unsatisfactory method, since it is practically impossible to apply opaque up to the edge of the image of the object without destroying the subtle values of edge and line. A good method is to raise a small object above the background and to work with diffuse or axis light.

Sunlight is especially favorable to photography of polished objects, such as silver or jewelry, because the reflections of the light source, being very intense, convey an impression of brilliancy. Secondary reflections, however, may be hard to manage unless the object is surrounded with smooth surfaces of low reflective value so that distracting secondary reflections are minimized. Complete elimination of secondary reflections is not desirable if the object is polished; the object is rendered far too dark except for the brilliant reflection of the light source. Again, if such an object is surrounded with reflective surfaces of continuous high value, the character of the substance may be distorted in the opposite way; a piece of silver, for example, may appear as brushed aluminum or worse, as plaster! Natural reflections are not always to be avoided; a silver ball, for instance, might very well show the reflections of clouds or trees, or even of figures or some stylized pattern of intentionally organized surfaces.

For photographing objects of intricate design and burnished surfaces, diffuse sunlight cannot be excelled. Stretching cheesecloth or mosquito netting above the subject at sufficient distance to destroy textural shadows gives a fine soft quality of light under which bright highlights are retained but are of somewhat broader quality than under direct sun. (In a strictly logical sense, modified sunlight might be called artificial light!)

Copying Paintings and Photographs

Anyone who has copied flat objects with artificial light knows the problems of getting even illumination and avoiding reflections. The use of sunlight or daylight for this purpose offers extraordinary advantages, and most excellent results are assured if certain environmental difficulties are overcome.

There is no problem with uneven lighting. Direct sunlight does not distort the color values of a painting, but light from the sky, being of a bluish cast, may lower the values of the reds and yellows and raise those of the blues. With black-and-white objects there is very little difference of effect between sunlight and skylight, and any type of negative material can be used. With paintings, panchromatic film is of course advised. Filters are helpful in clearing yellow stains and faded tones from photographs, etchings, etc.

As for the proper filters to use with paintings, that is a subject worthy of an entire book. The emotional impact of various colors—separately and in relation of other colors—is not conveyed in black-and-white values on a simple photometric-equivalent basis. With Type B Panchromatic Film in sunlight a K2 filter will give good standard "correction"; in skylight a minus-blue (No. 12) filter or a stereo-green (No. 55) filter will be found satisfactory. But these recommendations do not take into account the frequent need for nonrealistic interpretation of color values. To accent or to minimize certain colors we may resort to a variety of filters. To mention some:

G (15)	Lowers blue and blue-green, accentuates orange and red.
X1	Lowers red and blue, accentuates green.
B (58)	Severely lowers red and blue, accentuates green.
No. 38	Favors blue, lowers green and red.
E (23A)	Severely lowers green and blue, accentuates red.
A (25A)	Has a stronger effect than E.
C5	Severely lowers red and green, accentuates blue.

The saturation of the colors (as discussed in the section on Color (page 1) and the relative brightness of the color areas profoundly affect the black-and-white interpretation. I do not hesitate to say that *much* experience is necessary for adequate results in this field.

For those who are sufficiently interested in this field to devote much time and thought to it I suggest the three-filter technique described as follows:

1. Each of the 3 monochromats (A, red; B, green; and C5, blue) transmits its own color and excludes practically all the other colors. If their respective exposure factors are 8, 8, and 6, and if you expose a painting to each filter in turn (applying the full exposure factor for each filter), you will have a negative somewhat similar to that obtained from an unfiltered exposure, as each of the prime colors will be transmitted to the same value. The only difference in density would derive from the actual brightness of the color areas. However, due to the "overlap" of color transmission (the A filter transmits a little green, the B filter transmits a little red and blue, and the C5 filter transmits a little green) the actual exposure can be reduced about 1/3. If the calculated exposures with the A, B, and C5 filters were 24, 24, and 18 seconds, the actual exposures might be about 16, 16, and 12 seconds. I suggest making a test as follows:
   Make one exposure without filters.
   Make one exposure with filters (no compensation for overlap).
   Make one exposure with filters (compensating for overlap).
   Then compare for opacity effect.
2. However, you can fractionalize the exposure factors, giving less exposure with any one or two of the filters and thereby exert a very considerable control over the relative color values of the photograph.
3. Numerous systems have been presented for the relative exposures required for each of the three filters to balance properly the black-and-white interpretation of the painting, but as the personal factors are so involved I hesitate to present any of them here. My own approach is simply this:
   I make a negative using the green (B) filter only, and from that I make a print for study purposes. This print will show what emphasis is required for the red and blue components of the painting. Unless all colors of the painting are of very high saturation, the green filter will give a fair impression of the painting as a whole, and comparison of the print with the original subject will suggest the exposure required with the A and C5 filters.
4. Keep full records of every copy photograph, somewhat as follows:
   First negative
   a. Average brightness of painting in sunlight, 100 c.p.sq.ft.
   b. Placement of average brightness, Zone VI
   c. Exposure with panchromatic film of 50 speed at f/22 without filter, 1/6 sec.
   d. Exposure with B filter (8x), 8/6 (1⅓) sec.
   After analysis of the print, expose the second negative as follows:
   Second negative
   a. Figure basic exposure on placement of average brightness on Zone VI (light may change, but *placement* of measured values is important).
   b. Expose negative to varying times with the three filters one after the other—without jarring or moving camera or painting. For this purpose

it is best to use a shutter that operates on Bulb without requiring setting before each exposure. A Lux before-the-lens shutter is excellent.

Exposures: A, basic exposure x 6
              B, basic exposure x 8
              C5, basic exposure x 3

This would imply that both reds and blues should not be rendered in this case as high in value as the greens.

Your first attempts may not be successful, but after considerable experience you should be able to judge the desired proportions of the 3-filter control, and find making the first test negative seldom necessary.

The brightness range of most paintings is rather short; a vigorous watercolor only about 1:8, a strong painting about 1:10. These values were obtained with an S.E.I. meter, measuring areas about ½ inch across.

I find that in most cases if I place the average values on Zone VI or the highest values containing texture and color on Zone VII, I have a well-placed negative with sufficient "body." Underexposure gives weak and indefinite values. However, with very flat paintings I place the average values on Zone V and give the negative normal-plus development (about 1½x normal—see Book 2, p. 41). Too much contrast should be avoided.

In copying works of art it should be remembered that the object photographed is a complete esthetic expression; it is not a *subject* in the ordinary sense of the term. The photographer is ethically required to *transcribe* rather than freely interpret; hence he is obliged to respect the existing tonal values and relationships of the object.

The same principles of exposure apply to photographing black-and-white objects. Exposure-development control is always feasible with large-size negatives, but with 2¼x2¼ and smaller negatives the problem of grain is accentuated with more-than-normal development. Hence I advise that normal-plus development be given negatives 3¼x4¼ and larger; with negatives thus processed enlargements of from 3x to 5x can be made without disturbing grain effects appearing. (Even more than with natural objects, grain distorts the textural and surface qualities of paintings and other media photographically reproduced.)

With black-and-white photographs the lightest areas of the image can be placed on Zone VII, or, as in copying paintings, the average values can be placed on Zone VI. If increased contrast is required, place the average values on Zone V and give up to 1½x normal development. The Kodak Neutral Test Card (white side) can be used successfully for exposure determination as follows: With the card on the plane of the object photographed, place the measured brightness a little above Zone VII of the exposure scale, and compute the exposure accordingly.

Etchings, lithographs, drawings, etc., can be similarly treated, but their contrast is usually quite low, and care must be exercised not to produce a false contrast in the reproduction. Always work for a convincing quality in the whites and the high values to begin with. A good rendition of the paper on which they are made is important, but the paper textures should not be exaggerated.

In copying paintings and other examples of the graphic arts in natural light, the chief difficulty is environmental reflections; that is, reflections from surrounding objects and areas. The painting or other object being photographed should face a dark field, and bright reflective parts of the camera should be covered with dark paper or cloth if the object photographed is under glass or has a very highly varnished surface. The environmental reflections are not as important when the objects are photographed in sunlight as when photographed in shade; the proportion of the brightness of the reflections to the brightness of the sunlit object is quite low. But in shade, the environmental reflections can seriously degrade the brightnesses of the object. A painting with a high varnish, a photograph on glossy or semiglossy paper or one with obviously textured surface, will pick up diffuse reflections of the immediate environment, sometimes to such an extent that a definite sheen is observed over their surfaces. Hence back of the camera should be a sufficiently large dark area, such as a dark cloth or a large opening leading into a dark interior.

In any event, avoid glare from open sky or sun. The object photographed should be at an angle of not less than 45° to the direction of the light. However, the more acute the light, the more texture and unevenness of surface will be revealed. If paintings are in frames, be sure the frame does not cast a shadow on the painting itself.

Be certain the camera is properly oriented to the object—plane-of-negative parallel to plane-of-object. Otherwise distortions will appear—and there is nothing more slipshod than a nonrectangular photograph of a rectangular painting or photograph! As the axis of the lens is perpendicular to the plane of the object, the polarizer cannot be used. In Book 5 there is reference to how artificial lights may be polarized, thus permitting the use of polarizers before the lens with attendant removal of annoying reflections and minute highlights from the surfaces of varnished paintings and glossy photographs.

Objects can be copied near a window, but it is important to recognize the fact that the light falls off sharply from a window and uneven lighting of the object is almost inevitable—and very distressing! If a painting 4 feet wide is placed 6 feet from the light source, the brightness ratio of one edge to the other is 6^2 to 10^2, or about 1 to 3! A brightness differential of 1 to 1.5 can be quite disturbing in copies of paintings or photographs.

The intensity of the copying light should be considered. With artificial light we have a wide range of control, but with natural light we have the extreme intensity of sunlight on one hand, and a moderate value of skylight on the other hand. They are not consistent, especially if there are clouds in the sky. We can modify both by using diffusing screens and shields, etc. Or we can work indoors, using light from skylights and windows, etc., but always watchful that the light falling on our subject is evenly distributed. As the intensity of the illumination decreases the application of the reciprocity effect may be considered. Of course, as it is the intensity of the light *falling upon the film* that is the basis of the reciprocity effect, we can create it artificially by using very small stops and/or neutral density filters (see Book 1). Copying photographs in very low levels of illumination (or creating a low level of image intensity) will often give a more accurate interpretation of values. Likewise, copying photographs with speedlite also gives a good representative scale of values.

To sum up: Whenever possible, use direct sunlight for copying rather than skylight, but if you use the latter, be certain to shield the object from environmental reflections. And do not neglect to calculate for the additional exposure required for near objects if the lens is extended about one-eighth, or more, of its focal length at infinity setting.

PRE-EXPOSURE

Pre-exposure is described rather fully in Book 2 (pp. 109-10), but it is expedient to mention it again here if only to remind the reader that he has another means of controlling the contrast range of his subjects. Several chemicophysical means exist for increasing negative speed and extending the exposure scale, including subjecting the film to mercury vapor before exposure, making "masks," or giving the negative full or partial reduction or intensification. But to my mind the device of pre-exposure is one of the most effective methods of contrast control available and at the same time one of the simplest. It has been known for a long time among practical photographers that if you "shot the sky," that particular negative had greater "speed" and is superior for news and action photography under poor lighting conditions. In my early days in photography I recall making 1/200-second exposures of the open sky at f/22 and then using these negatives for difficult subjects in poor light. I had no idea of the technical significance of what I was doing; my approach was empirical, to say the least! I would now say that I was pre-exposing the sky on a Zone I placement—only now I can say definitely what I am doing, and in the earlier days I merely hoped it would "work."

A typical full-range subject (forest, figures, and snow) would benefit by pre-exposure, as the lowest brightnesses would be off the scale. Suppose the subject brightnesses are: (A) Shadow in trees, 6.5 c.p.sq.ft.; (B) dark tree trunks, 13; (C) shadow on figures, 50; (D) sun on figures, 400; (E) snow in sun, 1600; the following chart will show their relative positions on the exposure scale and the effect of pre-exposure to a Zone I value:

EFFECTS OF PRE-EXPOSURE

Zones:	O	I	II	III	IV	V	VI	VII	VIII	Brightness Range
Exposure units	(½)	(1)	(2)	(4)	(8)	(16)	(32)	(64)	(128)	1:256
Subject Brightnesses	6.5	13		50			400		1600	1:256
Same, in units	(½)	(1)		(4)			(32)		(128)	1:256
Pre-exposure units	(1)	(1)	(1)	(1)	(1)	(1)	(1)	(1)	(1)	1 unit only
Combined unit value	(1½)	(2)		(5)			(33)		(129)	1:86
Actual placement of effective values			A	B	C			D		E	1:86
Original placement of brightness values		A	B	C			D		E	1:256

The brightness range is reduced, but there is no practical effect on Zones VI and up.

As I said in Book 2: "Pre-exposure is thoroughly satisfactory for supporting small areas of shadow in which an impression of substance and texture is not imperative; but for large shadow areas it may show a false tonality, in which the appearance of a considerable area of uniform tone without texture or substance gives an illusion of allover fog."

114

46. The Grand Canyon (Infrared, from *My Camera in the National Parks*, Virginia Adams and Houghton Mifflin Co.)

INFRARED PHOTOGRAPHY

It is not my intention to do more than touch upon this subject, which is a large field in itself. However, I shall give a few suggestions applicable to the use of infrared in ordinary landscape work of expressive rather than technical objectives. My comments and suggestions are:

1. The usual exposure and development recommendations for optimum results with infrared film are based on a rather extreme contrast result, which to my way of thinking is often very unpleasant in the interpretative sense. Merely removing the air between the camera and a mountain range a hundred miles away—or photographing a green tree as plaster-white—does not necessarily achieve more than a superficial startling effect. However, in imaginative hands, I freely admit that magnificent departures from reality are possible.

2. I have had gratifying luck in using infrared film with a Wratten A filter, giving twice the recommended exposure and about 10 minutes' development in Kodak D-23 developer. This procedure yields great atmospheric clarity but avoids the extreme contrasts that obtain with conventional procedure.

3. I believe it best to avoid large areas of sky and water in the field of view, as these are inevitably rendered extremely dark. However, when you are photographing into the sun (see Figure 46, the Grand Canyon) the sky near the horizon will be rendered quite light in value.

4. For those interested in further applications of infrared I heartily recommend *Photography by Infrared,* by Walter Clark (John Wiley and Sons, N. Y.).

5. Some details of procedure:

a. Do not fail to extend lens-to-film distance a slight amount when using infrared film. Some lenses, such as the Ross Wide-angle Xpress, f/4, and the Cooke, Series XVI, are corrected for use with infrared and need no focus adjustment. Most miniature-camera lenses have a small index mark indicating the necessary adjustment of focus. In general, most lenses require an extension of from 1/75 to 1/200 of their focal length to compensate for the longer-than-visual wavelengths.

b. The ordinary exposure meters cannot be used with infrared film. The exposures recommended by the manufacturer are quite adequate for almost all conditions. (Note my personal recommendations above for doubling the exposure and giving soft development.)

c. Note that recommended exposures are for sunlit subjects; the exposure for objects in shadow is enormously long, as infrared rays have very feeble scattering power. Hence the extremely black shadows so apparent in ordinary work. However, when you are photographing into the sun, the distant shadows are supported by the intense atmospheric glare (again see Figure 46).

d. Do not keep infrared film in the holder long before exposing, and process as soon after exposure as possible.

47. Sierra Foothills, California. A G filter deepened the near-by shadows, but did not clear the distant sky.

INDEX

117

118